Composing Research, Communicating Results

Writing the Communication Research Paper

Writing is an aspect often overlooked in the quest to provide students with the necessary skills to embark on a career in the increasingly important field of communication. For many students, putting one's thoughts and understanding of a topic onto paper can be a daunting task. *Composing Research, Communicating Results: Writing the Communication Research Paper* provides communication students with the knowledge and necessary tools to compose a variety of course-required papers that are scholarly, accessible, and well-written. Chapter coverage includes common myths associated with writing a research paper, brainstorming and researching topics, making and supporting arguments, style and formatting issues, writing the literature review, application and personal reaction papers, empirical research papers, presenting and publishing your work, and more. Each stage of the process is broken down into easy-to-follow steps supported by writing exercises and numerous examples drawn from published and student-written papers in the field. *Composing Research, Communicating Results: Writing the Communication Research Paper* fulfils an important and underserved niche in the classroom curricula, and is an essential resource for all students in communications-related courses.

KURT LINDEMANN is Associate Professor and Director of Graduate Studies in the School of Communication at San Diego State University (SDSU). He also serves as the Director of the Center for the Study of Media and Performance, an interdisciplinary center at SDSU focused on the critical inquiry of live art and screen culture. Dr. Lindemann has taught courses in English composition, communication theory and methods, and more, and has published numerous scholarly and magazine articles, fiction, and poetry.

Composing Research, Communicating Results

Writing the Communication Research Paper

Kurt Lindemann

This edition first published 2018
© 2018 John Wiley & Sons, Inc

The right of Kurt Lindemann to be identified as the author of this work has been asserted in accordance with law.

Registered Offices
John Wiley & Sons, Inc., 111 River Street, Hoboken, NJ 07030, USA

Editorial Office
1606 Golden Aspen Drive, Suites 103 and 104, Ames, Iowa 50010, USA

For details of our global editorial offices, customer services, and more information about Wiley products visit us at www.wiley.com.

Wiley also publishes its books in a variety of electronic formats and by print-on-demand. Some content that appears in standard print versions of this book may not be available in other formats.

Library of Congress Cataloging-in-Publication data applied for

Hardback ISBN: 9781118940907
Paperback ISBN: 9781118940914

Cover image: Painting: "Winter Solstice" by Heather Sweeney
Photograph by Gregory Berg, Enso Photography
Cover design by Wiley

Set in 10/12pt Warnock by SPi Global, Pondicherry, India
Printed and bound in Malaysia by Vivar Printing Sdn Bhd

10 9 8 7 6 5 4 3 2 1

I dedicate this book to my writing and communication teachers, and to my writing and communication students, who have all taught me the value of critical thinking, self-expression, and a genuine connection with others in the process of better understanding each other and the world around us.

Contents

Contents

Preface

In my years teaching composition and communication classes, I've come to realize that writing and communication have several things in common. The first is
that, because we often do both on a daily basis – writing e-mails, texting, talking
to others – we generally assume we know how to do them. This isn't always the
case. Unfortunately, because we engage in written and oral communication so
often, we tend to become *mindless* about them. We might develop bad habits, or
we might think that just because we communicate one way with some people,
that particular way of communicating is appropriate and effective for other people as well. The second thing I realized is that we tend to think good writers, like
good public speakers, are simply born that way.

I developed this book to respond to these two myths. First, I hope to make
readers of this book more *mindful* about their writing choices and understand
that different audiences sometimes require different styles of writing. Second,
I hope to provide readers with the knowledge and skills to make these mindful
choices. I believe good writers, like good public speakers, are *made* that way with
proper instruction and, of course, a lot of practice.

This book draws on my years of teaching college composition and working in
college writing centers, and teaching communication classes in which writing
assignments constitute a major part of the class. I present lessons I've learned as
a teacher and writer, as well as sage advice from others who are smarter (and better writers) than me. I also offer samples of writing assignments from my own
students to help illustrate the concepts in each chapter.

- **Chapter 1** introduces the book, discusses some of the major challenges of
  writing class papers, offers and then debunks some myths about writing, and
  presents a "Tao" of writing that encompasses topic, audience, and occasion. It
  also presents some guidelines for other types of writing you may do beyond
  class assignments.
- **Chapter 2** presents some tried-and-true brainstorming techniques, a more in-
  depth consideration of audience, and a discussion of the types of questions that
  might be posed in class papers and how those questions can help formulate a
  plan for conducting library and database research.
- **Chapter 3** discusses the role of argument in writing class papers, provides an
  in-depth consideration of the Toulmin Method of constructing arguments,
  and reviews some of the more common citation styles for class papers.

- **Chapter 4** revists the concept of audience in a consideration of first-, second-, and third-person voice, as well as active and passive voice. It also discusses the "flow" of a paper and how to ensure smooth writing and eliminate "filler" from papers using my own TESLA Method of paragraph construction. The chapter concludes with a discussion of style and some common grammar mistakes.
- **Chapters 5, 6, and** 7 provide overviews of some more common paper assignments in social science and communication classes: the literature review, application and reaction paper, and empirical research paper, respectively.
- **Chapter 8** offers a "dos and don'ts" list for presenting the finished paper in public speaking settings, including a discussion of submitting papers to local, regional, national, and international conferences and journals.

Each chapter has several features to help readers better understand and utilize the concepts discussed. The "Write Away" feature offers easy-to-follow exercises to immediately put into practice the tips, guidelines, and advice presented. "Building Blocks" are meant to break up the writing of the paper into short tasks that, if done thoughtfully, will help to produce a well-written final paper. "Engaging Ethics" sections provide a consideration of some ethical dangers associated with a particular aspect of writing – from citing sources to submitting to conferences – and how to avoid them. The "Student Spotlight" boxes present writing samples from real students to illustrate certain ideas, concepts, methods, and techniques.

For Instructors

Communication skills are considered a necessity, but written communication skills are sometimes overlooked, especially in communication classes. Not all communication students will complete a senior paper or thesis, but writing in communication classes is an integral part of assessment. Most communication instructors assign papers, but many lack the time to revisit writing and composition practices in their courses.

This book, geared toward upper-division undergraduate and Master's-level graduate students, draws on actual, student-written examples from common paper assignments to provide students with the knowledge and tools to compose course papers in a scholarly, accessible, and well-written manner. Covering all aspects of the writing process, including brainstorming, creating and supporting arguments, and common types of class papers (literature reviews, application and reaction, empirical research), this book is designed to work in conjunction with any communication or social science course, and can supplement any required communication textbook.

For Students

Writing is sometimes a mystery. You're at a keyboard, in front of a screen, staring down at a blank piece of paper, and then, somehow, the words come to you. Or, they don't, at least not right away. Maybe you think, "I do my best work under pressure. If I write the paper the night before it's due, the words seem to flow more easily." Or maybe you think, "What's the difference? I won't use any of these skills after I'm done with this class anyway." This book desmystifies this process so you're better prepared before you start writing, have a plan when you're writing, and know what to do if the words don't come.

And I'm not the only one helping you along on this journey. You also have advice and examples from other students who were once in the same position you are. Working together, we can make this journey you're on less like a mystery and more like an adventure, or at least a journey with a destination and a map to help you get there.

Acknowledgments

Writing is often a solitary activity, but there are still people who help shape your paper, book, or article, and who have helped shaped you as an author. In this case, there are many people I must acknowledge for their help with this book, as well as for the impact they've had on me as a writer.

I'd like to thank all the folks previously and currently at Wiley-Blackwell for their help with all stages of this book: Mark Graney, Julia Kirk, Haze Humbert, Elizabeth Swayze, Milos Vuletic, and Liz Wingett. Additionally, I have immense gratitude for Janet Moth for her keen editorial eye. Thanks also goes to Shyamala Venkateswaran for help with the production process. Finally, a big thanks to Maddie Koufogazos for marketing and help with the book cover concept.

The cover art itself is taken from a painting by the immensely talented Heather Sweeney, photographed by Gregory Berg at Enso Photography. While one shouldn't judge a book by its cover, I hope that borrowing their artistic endeavors for this book cover makes it easier for readers to judge this book a success!

I had the pleasure of learning from several creative and non-fiction writing teachers in the Department of English Language and Literature at Eastern Michigan University, as well as from many of the excellent professors in the Hugh Downs School of Human Communication at Arizona State University, including Sarah Tracy and Linda Park-Fuller. Additionally, I had the good fortune of having some great colleagues serve as reviewers for the initial manuscript of this book. Other colleagues in the Communication discpline, including those at San Diego State University, also provided invaluable support and encouragement. Thank you all.

Perhaps the biggest thank you goes to my students. Their desire and willingness to take risks in their writing, to work diligently on their writing, and to lend me their voices for the purpose of teaching others has truly made this book a one-of-a-kind text I hope readers (students and teachers alike) will find valuable in their own writing endeavors.

Kurt Lindemann

1

So You *Have* to Write a Research Paper …

Chapter Learning Outcomes

- Identify Myths about Writing Research Papers
- Distinguish Types of Papers Commonly Written
- Identify the Purposes of Different Research Papers
- Apply Writing Skills to "Real-World" Texts

Composing Research, Communicating Results: Writing the Communication Research Paper,
First Edition. Kurt Lindemann.
© 2018 John Wiley & Sons, Inc. Published 2018 by John Wiley & Sons, Inc.

Chapter Features

- "Write Away"
- Building Blocks

You are sitting in a cramped chair facing the front of the classroom. You look around the classroom and listen to the low chatter of students awaiting the start of class. Some faces and voices are familiar, others are not. You look forward to making new friends, talking to people with different experiences and ideas, and maybe learning something. You hope to get a good grade, too, of course. You check your phone for the time. Class is about start. The teacher enters the room: pleasant demeanor, conversational tone, funny. This might just be a fun class, you think. Then the teacher begins to explain the assignments for the upcoming term. The major one, the assignment upon which most of your grade rests: a research paper. Why?, you think. Why a research paper? You re-evaluate the class and the teacher. Suddenly, all the positive things you initially thought about the class seem, well ... not so positive.

The above scenario is likely a common one in many students' experiences. The course research paper, sometimes called a "term paper," is an object of much derision, disdain, and dread among students. And, certainly, writing a research paper is *difficult*. Writing a *good* research paper is even *more difficult*. I'm not writing this book to convince you otherwise. I do, however, think that, with some knowledge and skills, almost anyone can succeed in writing a good research paper. Some people think that good writers are born not made, that somehow – genetically blessed or with gifts granted by a divine being – some people just *get* writing. I do not believe this. Sure, some folks have an easier time writing papers; I'm not denying that. But I think that good writers can be *made*; otherwise, I wouldn't be writing this book. And you probably don't think good writers are born, not made; otherwise you wouldn't be reading this book. Of course, it's entirely possible you're reading this because your teacher required you to read it. If this is the case, then at least your teacher probably thinks the same as I do.

What This Book Is Not ...

Here's what this book is not. While we will explore some common grammar mistakes, this is not a text on proper grammar and sentence diagramming. While we will talk about integrating scholarly and popular literature into a research paper, this is not a how-to on library research, nor is it a summary of relevant communication and social science research. While I will provide some easy-to-remember steps to completing commonly assigned papers, this is not a fill-in-the-blank template for outlines and papers.

What This Book Is ...

I admit that I had selfish reasons for writing this book. I am a Professor of Communication at a university. I teach research methods, performance studies, organizational communication, and a few other courses. I regularly assign research papers to my undergraduate and graduate students. And while I have a Ph.D. in communication, I also have a graduate degree in English language and literature, which required me to teach English composition classes and work in the department's writing tutoring center. As a result, much to my current students' dismay, I found myself frequently commenting on sentence structure, topic sentence usage, grammar mistakes, and other writing issues. I found myself writing the same comments time and again. I began to think, "It would be great if there were a book that collected all these comments and explained them for students." Shortly after thinking this, I began writing this book.

That said, this book isn't meant to replace the instruction from your own teacher. It is meant to help guide you through a sometimes daunting and intimidating process. This book is not meant to convince you to *like* writing papers. If you don't already, chances are a textbook isn't going to change your mind. What this book *is* intended to do is to make the writing process easier and to help ensure the entire writing process results in successful outcomes: well-written arguments and analysis and ... oh, yeah, possibly a *good grade*!

Features of This Book

As you read this book, you'll find several features I think will be helpful in understanding the concepts and practices covered in each chapter. The first are "Write Away" boxes that offer writing exercises you can immediately put into practice to improve your writing. "Building Blocks" are meant to be short "mini assignments" which, once completed, you can integrate into your larger writing assignment. Research papers are fraught with ethical challenges, from plagiarizing to improperly citing sources. For this reason, the "Engaging Ethics" feature provides some things to consider to better avoid the ethical pitfalls that may arise in the course of your research and writing. Finally, since we often learn best from our peers, the "Student Spotlight" sections provide actual examples of student writing that illustrate the concepts and assignments covered in this book. Each feature should not only help you better understand the concepts we cover in this book, they should also help you *write* better.

The Purpose of This Chapter

So, we "begin at the beginning," as the King instructs the White Rabbit in *Alice's Adventures in Wonderland* (Carroll 1920, 182). This chapter is a beginning: the first step, the first brick in a sidewalk path, the first word in a sentence, the first page of a book. No better place to start. And this is true for writing papers as well.

> Put one word after another. Find the right word, put it down.
>
> *Neil Gaiman (2014)*

This chapter will first try to debunk some myths about writing. Mental blocks are the most difficult obstacles to writing well; you can always learn proper sentence structure and new words, but it's much harder to learn to *unthink* solidified beliefs. As such, we'll address some of these commonly held beliefs or myths. Then we'll review some of the major types of papers commonly assigned, which I'll also cover in detail in subsequent chapters. Finally, we'll discuss how the skills you gain from these assignments can transfer to other types of writing you might do in the "real world."

We'll start with some commonly held beliefs or myths about writing papers for class. I'll reframe as *challenges* what we might normally think of as *chores*. After that, we'll move on to myths specific to composing research papers, ones that I've heard students (and some professors!) say over and over again.

Writing Papers: Chore or Challenge?

In this section, we'll discuss challenges to writing well, writing efficiently, and to just plain writing. This last part is important because simply writing – writing anything – is sometimes the best way to start. The questions that begin each of the following sections are common ones asked by all types of writers, from students to professionals. While I attempt to *respond* to each question, I don't always provide *answers*. Instead, I try to offer different ways to think about each question, framing them as challenges that can be overcome rather than chore-filled drudgery.

Challenge: How do I find time to write?

Let's face it, writing a paper – even poorly – can take a lot of time. It can easily become a time-consuming task. This is, I argue, true and false. Certainly, writing can take a lot of time. No one will write your papers for you; *you* must put one word in front of the other. However, viewing the writing process as a series of small time chunks instead of 10 pages you have to write in one night can make the task seem more manageable. This isn't a secret. Many writers have come to this conclusion, as the Neil Gaiman quote earlier in this chapter illustrates. Similarly, novelist Henry Miller (1964) said, "If you can't create, you can *work*" (161).

Just write. Put one word in front of the other until you've created a sentence. It certainly sounds simple, doesn't it? So, what's the best way to go about it? Of course, that depends on your schedule, but regardless of your schedule, a few things are clear from the wisdom of the writers previously quoted. First:

• Make a schedule for writing. Don't wait for "inspiration."

A common phrase I hear from students over and over goes something like this: "I do my best writing under pressure. The words just seem to flow better." What these students end up doing is waiting until the last possible moment, often the night before the paper is due, to begin writing a paper they probably should have started weeks before. This process *might* get that student a passing grade. Compared to some other students, his or her paper might actually seem pretty good. But this attitude will only take someone so far. Eventually, especially in upper-division classes or, after graduation, with a big project for work, he or she is in for a rude awakening. More time will be required for increasingly important projects.

Of course, there are many reasons why someone might wait until the last minute. She may not feel like she has the time to devote to the paper. It may be a matter of weighing the costs and rewards: he might be afraid that if he puts all that time into a paper and doesn't get an A, it makes more sense to devote less time for a similar grade. Either way, though, waiting until the last minute causes undue stress and doesn't give you the time needed to properly edit your writing. Yes, you read that correctly: "edit." One saying of which I'm fond is, "How do I know what I want to say until I've seen what I said?" Translation: writing and editing a first draft is important. When you wait until the last minute, you may not leave yourself enough time to edit your paper.

Starting the writing process earlier, making a schedule, and blocking out time for writing can help you leave yourself time to edit. For example, I find I'm usually receptive to writing in the morning, so I will often sit down to write at around 6:30 or 7:00 a.m. Pick a time that's good for you. But I don't mean to simply prolong the agony and stress by starting earlier. You need to give yourself a break so you don't feel chained to your desk, chair, or laptop. So, along with a starting time for your writing, set an end time as well. I set an end time, around 8:30 or 9:00 a.m. At that point, I finish up whatever sentence I'm writing, make some notes about what might come next, and I leave it. Of course, you'll have to work around your own schedule, but carving out a half-hour well in advance of the due date can be helpful in the long run.

But what happens during this time we've blocked out? How do we know what to write? Our writers above give us some points on that as well. To summarize:

- Put one word in front of the other. If you don't feel "inspired," do it anyway.

Fantasy and fiction writer Neil Gaiman (2014) advises us: "Write. Put one word after another. Find the right word, put it down." Henry Miller admonishes, "When you can't *create* you can *work*." What do these two have in common? Simple. Sit down and write. You may not like what comes out at first. What you write may not end up in your final paper. But, as obvious as it sounds, in order to write a paper *you have to write*.

Remember that this section is about finding the time to write. Our discussion up to this point is useful because sometimes we imagine that writing is a marathon-long process of inspiration. In reality, as unromantic as it sounds, it's *work*. Or, rather, it can be thought of as work when you're just not "feeling it." When all

---

Write Away

Make a schedule to write. Include time set aside for brainstorming, Internet and online database research, and outlining. Then, divide up your time by committing yourself to write a certain number of pages during a specific time period. Start with one double-spaced page in half an hour. That may seem like a lot, or it may seem like not enough. Regardless, stop yourself to see where you are after half an hour and adjust accordingly. Do this for two weeks.

   If you block out one day of the week for research and outlining, and commit to writing for half an hour on three other days of the week, you could potentially have a total of six pages of a first draft of your paper in two weeks. Your assignment might be shorter than this, or perhaps it's a little longer, so be sure to plan out several weeks before the due date. Once you've finished the draft of your paper, you should have a lot of time to revise and edit. Try it!

---

else fails, treat it as a job: you clock in, put in your time working (whether it be a half-hour or an hour), and then you clock out and leave the work "at work." At the end of the process, you will have more quality pages than if you wait for inspiration to strike you the night before the paper is due. How? Because you will have left yourself time to revise your draft!

Challenge: Is this supposed to be fact or opinion?

So, you've made the time to write by creating a schedule and sticking to it. What do you write? While that question is best answered by your instructor, I will address a common question about content I get from students all the time: "Is my paper supposed to be *fact* or *opinion*?" We'll discuss this conundrum further in Chapter 3: Making Arguments, Providing Support. But let's briefly explore this question below.

   First, let's get this binary out of our minds. When it comes to research papers for your classes, fact and opinion are not two opposing things; they are one and the same. More specifically, your opinion should be supported with "facts" derived from research. That's really what an argument is, after all: an author's educated opinion about something skillfully supported with the use of "facts."

   Second, allow me to explain why I'm placing "facts" in quotation marks. Although we often use facts as support, the broader term *evidence* is a better word to describe what we use to bolster our arguments. As I've told my public speaking students again and again, the term "facts" conjures up statistics to many students. And as any public speaking textbook will tell you, statistics are not the only – or the best – way to support an argument. Even with this in mind, the use of "facts" in a paper can present a problem.

   When student writers first encounter research papers, argumentative papers, or any written assignment in which they have to make a claim based on a synthesis of reading, they often use a massive number of direct quotations. If these quotations are cited correctly, there's *technically* nothing wrong with this. But the more one quotes directly, the less likely these quotations will explicitly provide support for an argument. Why? Because, with many beginning student writers at least, direct quotations are less likely to be synthesized into an argument and woven into a paper seamlessly. The tendency of many student writers is to just drop these quotations in at places that seem logical, with little effort made to link the quotations to the broader argument. The authors from whom we quote cannot make the arguments for us; we have to do that in our own words.

The short answer to the question above, then, is that your paper should be *both* fact *and* opinion.

Challenge: How do I find research on my topic?

Okay. You've made the time to write. You also have a better idea of the differences between your opinion and the evidence you use to support your opinion. But you need to find the evidence you're going to use as support, and you need to know how to find it. This brings us to another challenge facing many student writers: finding research on a topic. We'll address this process more in Chapter 2: Brainstorm and Research. For now, let's demystify this challenge a little bit.

Since you now understand a little better that your papers are your *opinions supported with evidence*, it should be easier to grasp the idea that no one author has published any article in the wide world of online and print sources that argues exactly what you are arguing. And if they have, then you should think about altering your claim – they said it first, they've got "dibs," and you don't want to argue exactly what someone else has already argued.

In supporting your opinion – something I will refer to as your argument or, more specifically, your *claim* from here on out – you need to make the sources *work for you*, not organize your paper based only on a narrow body of literature related to your study. For example, if you're arguing that effective interpersonal communication is hindered by social media, you can search for research on social media, and you can search for research on interpersonal communication. However, you can also search for research on friendships, romantic relationships, and familial relationships.

Ultimately, keyword searches with creative, out-of-the-box brainstorming will be key to overcoming the challenge of finding sources. With some of the techniques offered in Chapter 2, this will seem less daunting – and even fun!

Challenge: Problems and potential of using published articles as models

Even the most creative brainstorming isn't enough to give you an idea of how to put your paper together. The most obvious place to look for examples of well-written academic papers is the published research articles you're gathering to use as evidence for your own paper. But be aware, there are advantages and disadvantages of using these pieces as models for your own paper.

Let's address the advantages first. A lot of communication articles are written to adhere to particular publishing conventions. In later chapters, I'll admonish you to avoid the passive voice (for example, "This research was conducted to investigate…" and "Significance was found…"), yet many articles are written in the passive voice. Why is this? In the case of these particular articles, the communication *paradigm*, or way of viewing the world (Kuhn 1962), in which the researchers are working views truth and reality as objective and external to researchers. The paradigm in which you might find many instances of the passive voice is sometimes called the Functionalist (Burrell and Morgan 1979), Sociopsychological (Craig 1999), or Discovery paradigm (Merrigan and Huston 2015). It might also simply be called a Social Scientific paradigm. In any case, the authors working in this paradigm value "good science" and don't believe it matters who is conducting the study. As such, the first person "I" is usually removed from the reporting of the research. This particular viewpoint often leads to the use of the passive voice, something you should avoid in your own papers unless instructed otherwise.

Another problem with using published articles as models, of course, is that the articles you find when conducting research are often written by professors. This means: (a) they have more experience and knowledge about that phenomenon than do you; (b) they likely have more time than you do to write their essays, or (c) they probably get paid to write (many, not all, professors get release time to do research and publish). These last two factors make a big difference in being able to write good research articles. So, while you may want to use these articles as a model for your own paper, remember that the authors have access to resources you might not yet be able to access.

Building Blocks

Using published research as models for your own research paper can be a successful strategy, if done smartly and realistically. My poetry teacher, Clayton Eshleman, once said to our graduate class, "The best way to study a poem is to copy it." He didn't mean copy it word for word; he meant try and capture the flow of the piece, to understand how it works, and then try to reproduce that in your own poem. For example, he recommended using the same number of syllables and the same number of lines in the same number of stanzas. That way, he said, we could better study a poem that we emulated and learn about the writing process (and our writing) at the same time. I offer similar advice for using published research as a model.

1) Pick a published article or essay you like. You might also choose a student paper your teacher has presented as exemplary.
2) Determine how many paragraphs the authors use in their literature review. What are they trying to accomplish in that section? Try to do the same thing in yours. And so on. Let's be clear: I'm not encouraging you to plagiarize any part of the published article you're using as a model. We'll talk more about plagiarism in Chapter 3.

3) Adapt this process as necessary to your own class assignments. If your paper is only a literature review, chances are your paper will be longer than the literature review in the published article (those authors had to make room for their findings and conclusions). But you get the idea.

Table 1.1 The myths of writing debunked

Myth	Debunked
"I don't have time to write."	If you make the time, you will have the time.
"Too much editing breaks up my flow."	You'll only know if the paper "flows" or makes sense if you read it after you've written it and edit when necessary.
"I don't need to outline. It's all in my head."	You'll only know what want to say *after* you see what you've said (or written).
"Writing papers is a useless skill."	Written communication skills are consistently among the top skills employers desire in employees.

In this first section, I've tried to reframe many of "chores" associated with writing a research paper – finding time to write, finding the main purpose, finding research, and findings models to emulate – as challenges to be overcome. However, it's also important to reconsider some myths we might have about research papers (see Table 1.1).

Debunking Myths about Research Papers

The first myth is easily dispelled, as it's much of what we've already covered:

• Myth #1: "I don't have time to write."

Simply, if you make the time, you will have the time. When many students think of "time" to write, they imagine themselves blocking out several hours at a time. This is often because they wait until the last minute. Using the strategies outlined in the previous section, you won't have to wait until the last minute. Therefore, your blocks of writing time will be considerably shorter.

The second myth is related to the first:

• Myth #2: "Too much editing breaks up my flow."

Ah, yes. The elusive "flow" of a paper, something many students talk about but for which they can never seem to provide a precise definition. In Chapter 4: Style and Format, I attempt to give a shape and understanding to what this "flow" really is. For now, let's not worry about it. Instead, let's worry more about whether the paper itself *makes sense*. How do we know if it makes sense? We have to read it. When do we read it? The same time we read anything: *after it's been written*. This means, of course, that you can't read something while you're writing it. Of course, you're reading your paper as you write it. But it's difficult to tell if the sentence you're writing is coherent in the context of the paper when you haven't even finished the paper. Organizational communication theorist Karl Weick (1995) put it best when he asked, "How do I know what I think before I see what I said?" (12). In short, you need to have written something first *before* you know if it's truly what you wanted to write.

Luckily, you don't have to write the entire paper to be able to tell if what you've written is really what you want to say. In addition to re-reading each section of your paper after you've written it, you can also jot down a general idea of what you want to say. However, this ability to *forecast* your paper without writing it sentence for sentence in its entirety requires us to debunk another myth:

- Myth #3: "I don't need to outline. It's all in my head."

Outlining is a useful but little-used tool for writing papers. Yes, it requires some extra preparation work. However, this "extra work" (I put this phrase in quotations because I don't consider it extra but a common part of writing any paper) in advance of writing the paper will make for a stronger paper later on.

If you subscribe to this myth and really believe it, I'm sure you've already dismissed all the various metaphors about outlining you may have heard in your other writing classes: outlining is the like the foundation for a building; outlining is the spine of the paper; and so on. I prefer to return to a tale commonly attributed to Karl Weick, but one that first appeared in a poem by scientist (and part-time poet) Miroslav Holub (Gellman and Basbøll 2013). This poem recounts a tale of Hungarian soldiers lost in the Alps. They faced certain death, until one soldier discovered a map and used it to lead the platoon to safety. Only after they were out of harm's way did they realize that they had a map of the Pyrenees, not the Alps.

What does this story mean? Well, the map was useful even though it didn't accurately represent their journey. When you make an outline, you create a map. Your journey may change, sure; you may end up writing a paper that's different from the outline. But, similar to the soldiers in the poem, you need some kind of outline – a map of some sort – to begin your journey in the first place. This tale about the Hungarian soldiers is considered a great source for the theory and practice of leadership, in part because of what it represents. Leaders can apply the saying "The map is not the territory" to get their employees or followers started on what may seem like a difficult journey. The applicability of this idea helps to dispel the last myth we're going to debunk.

Writing papers can seem like busy work, and many students intone the same mantra over and over in their resistance to such assignments:

- Myth #4: "Writing papers is a useless skill."

We now know from the story above that the practice of writing well-thought-out papers has skills transferable to the realms of leadership and management. Other transferable skills include: argumentation, synthesis of others' ideas, time management, research skills, and… writing. Many employers point to writing and communication skills as some of the most important an employee should possess (Eatherington 2015; O'Farrell 2015). In other words, writing papers is not a "useless" skill. Although outlining, writing paragraphs here and there, and compiling bibliographies may seem like busy work, they all require skills that will prove useful later on.

The "Tao" of Writing

Whether the writing you're doing is for a general audience online or in hard copy, or for more specific groups of people, remembering the "Tao" of professional writing will serve you well, especially as you begin to write *beyond* the classroom. The word "Tao" signifies a Chinese concept that often means the way of, path of, road to, or guiding principles of something. The Tao of Writing, then, is a way or path to good writing. I use the term here because it is also an acronym for what I believe are the three components of good writing: Topic, Audience (or readers), and Occasion (Figure 1.1). I address each of these components below. Whether in the context of a common class assignment or a common type of professional writing, writers must account for each of these components if their ideas are to be communicated clearly and effectively.

Topic

The topic about which you're writing, whether you choose it or it's given to you, determines a lot about the *way* you should write. Granted, you want to choose a topic that interests you and will sustain your interest throughout the duration of writing your paper. But you also want to write what people, and especially your teachers who are grading your papers, *want* to read.

Audience

Speaking of which, who is reading your paper? For a class paper, it's your teacher, of course. But is that the extent of your audience of readers? Obviously, you should write with some awareness of your teacher as your reader because you, like most students, probably want to write a good paper to get a good grade. But what does your teacher want to read about? What do they already know about the topic? What about a more general audience of readers? In most cases, your instructors probably want you to write for this general audience. But with that consideration comes a whole host of other concerns: the use of slang, pop culture references, and detailed versus truncated explanations of theories, for example. While there's no one correct way to write a paper, thinking about your audience is the second step, and naturally flows from a consideration of your topic.

Occasion

Just as you might have learned in public speaking classes, the *reason* you're writing your paper is important to consider. Rather than just thinking about writing because you have to, or to get a good grade, think about the

Figure 1.1 The "TAO" of Writing: Topic, Audience, Occasion

purpose of your paper in a way more related to audience: to explain a concept, to critique an artifact (film, book, advertisement, etc.), or to persuade your audience about something.

These three elements – topic, audience, and occasion – comprise the TAO of writing, the pathway to good writing. And each is important to take into account, whether you're writing papers for class or writing other documents more relevant to your professional career. In the pages that follow, I cover some common types of writing in the academic and professional realms.

Types of Papers

What types of papers should you expect in your classes? Your instructor's syllabus will be the most important document to help you determine this. But you may be asked to write other, similar types of papers in other classes. Below, I provide brief summaries of the types of papers you may find yourself writing at one point or another in your academic career.

Reviews of literature

This is probably the most common type of paper you'll find yourself writing. This type of paper is so ubiquitous among college classes, I've devoted an entire chapter to it (Chapter 5: Writing the Literature Review). It may appear easy, but it's the most difficult paper to write. It's difficult because, on the surface, it appears to be simply a non-biased reporting of what others have researched and written regarding a particular topic. That sentence just sounded boring, didn't it? Imagine writing or, worse yet (at least for your teachers), *reading* such a paper.

Thankfully, a review of literature, sometimes called a "state of the art" paper, isn't merely a reporting of others' work; it's an *argument* you make about a body of research. For example, imagine you're assigned a literature review in an interpersonal communication class. You decide to research "friends with benefits" (believe it or not, there's been a lot of communication research done on this topic), or friends who may also have a sexual relationship. Your task for the paper shouldn't just be to tell your audience what others have found regarding this topic. Instead, it should be to support an original argument. Your thesis sentence – the point of your paper summarized in one sentence (more on thesis sentences in Chapter 4) – could be something as simple as, "While the research on 'friends with benefits' has been plentiful, it has yet to account for the changing face of romantic relationships, including those between same-sex and transgendered people." Or it could be, "The extant research on 'friends with benefits', while enhancing our understanding of certain types of relationships, should evolve to include the role technology plays in such relationships." Notice that in each instance, an argument is forwarded: as in, "the research doesn't account for this," or "our current understanding could be strengthened by including something else." In Chapter 3, we'll discuss arguments in more detail. For now, imagine someone asking you the question "Why?" in response to each thesis. Your literature review then becomes a series of *reasons* why your thesis is true, supported with the scholarly literature about and related to your topic, as well as any other type of literature (popular press, magazines, newspapers, etc.) approved by your instructor. Granted, these thesis sentences aren't earth-shattering, save-the-world types of arguments, but it makes for a review of literature that is ultimately more interesting than a simple summary of what others have found.

This skill of creating compelling arguments is just one of many skills transferable across papers and, as discussed earlier, to any number of occupations. You'll soon realize that a *claim-evidence* (thesis-support) formula is common across all the papers you'll likely be expected to write. Not surprisingly, the next type of paper I cover also functions as an argument, but in a more obvious way.

Analysis, application, and reaction papers

In addition to the review of literature, the analysis, application, or reaction paper is probably the most commonly assigned in communication courses and other similar courses (sociology, film, and media, for example). As is evident from the names of these types of papers, you will be expected to argue and support with evidence your opinion on something, usually some kind of artifact (advertisement, article, movie, etc.). We'll talk more about these papers in Chapter 6: Application and Reaction Papers. But just as I discussed earlier, this paper, like the literature review, is both fact *and* opinion. It is an argument of your educated opinion supported with examples taken from the artifact and analyzed with theoretical concepts.

Empirical research papers

These papers usually require students to gather data themselves, whether the data is from a survey, interviews, field observations, a rhetorical artifact (speech, advertising campaign, etc.), or perhaps a mix of all of them. While the formatting may be different for each "genre" of study (quantitative, ethnographic, rhetorical, cultural studies, etc.), the goal of each paper remains the same as for the others we've discussed: to make claims and support them with evidence. The beauty of an empirical research paper is that it incorporates parts of each of the previous papers we've already covered: a review of literature and some kind of analysis. While an original, data-driven research paper can seem intimidating, you already probably know about it than you realize.

Each of type or genre of research paper has its own conventions, which may make this type of paper confusing. Later in this book, we'll address the various types of data-driven research papers you may find yourself asked to write, and I'll offer some helpful tips on *how* to write for each one. Once you know the "tricks" of each – for example, some are commonly written in the third person, some in the first person, some require attention to figures of speech, some frame writing more as a report of what was found in the study rather than as shaping a reader's understanding of the study itself (confusing – see what I mean?) – you'll be able to approach each more confidently.

Thinking Beyond the Paper – Writing for a Professional Career

We've already debunked the myth that writing is a useless skill. And we've already addressed the fact that employers consistently report that communication skills, speaking *and* writing, are a priority in new hires. But you still may be wondering *how* you might apply these newly acquired writing skills. Well, you don't have to be a professional writer to encounter on-the-job opportunities to write.

It should come as no surprise, especially to those of you who are communication majors, that communication is one of the skills most sought after by employers because communication is omnipresent in the workplace. We're frequently called upon to communicate with others, whether they are customers in a restaurant, students in a classroom, work team members, or clients and colleagues in the virtual world. It's this last example of online communication that has bolstered the importance of good writing. With no face-to-face component, writing is the sole way you get your message across in online forums. Below are a few examples of the types of writing you might be called upon to do in the workplace.

Handbooks and manuals

Manuals are perhaps the most obvious type of workplace writing you may encounter. I don't mean writing owners' manuals for cars, although that might be the case. If you are a manager in any capacity, you may be called upon to write a training manual for new employees. Such manuals regarding how to do things at work are often ignored by employees in favor of informal communication with other workers (Eisenberg, Goodall, and Trethewey 2015; Pacanowsky and O'Donnell-Trujillo 1983). Of course, employee handbooks that cover legal issues, rights, and the responsibilities of the company and employees should be read thoroughly. But how-to manuals (or sections of an employee handbook) might be a different story. Obviously, you want your new employees to read every page thoroughly. Although they may not consider it a must-read bestseller à la Stephen King, it follows that the better written it is, the more likely they are to read it. Additionally, customers and clients may also need manuals for accompanying products and services.

So, what makes a well-written manual? Some experts argue that authors of manuals need to know their objective, outline it first, be brief, be clear, and use examples (Messmer 2012). Of course, it depends on the content, but ultimately manuals benefit from a clear and concise expression of ideas. Such clarity may include a number of things one learns in a public speaking class (and which I'll address later in Chapter 4): previews, reviews, transitions, examples, memorable language relevant to the topic, and a reasonable length to enable comprehension.

Policy manuals, vision statements, and mission statements

Another common type of writing you may find yourself practicing outside the classroom is the writing of documents, passages, and entries that attempt to define an organization's stance, procedures, and goals: specifically policy, mission, and vision statements. You may be doing this in an official capacity for an organization as an executive officer, a public relations professional, as an internal communications officer, or maybe even as a communication consultant. Who knows, you may also be doing this for your own start-up business!

Policy statements differ from mission and vision statements in the level of specificity. Generally, policy statements are more concrete and "practical" in that they provide organizational members' guidelines. Like some manuals, then, policy statements are written for a specific audience. Unlike manuals, which may have a step-by-step guide for doing something, policy statements are written to provide a general overview of a particular rule, law, or written norm (UC-Davis). For policy statements, remember that the readers will, you hope, return to your document again and again for reference (and you also hope, if you're serving as your organization's Human Resources person, instead of asking you!). So, policy manuals need to be clear, concise, and written with the old adage in mind that "less is more." If you want people to actually *use* the policy manual, then you must make it *user*-friendly.

Mission and vision statements are different from policy manuals, and are similar to yet different from each other. First, let's go over the similarities among mission and vision statements. Both are written for a general audience. With policy statements, your readers are already organizational members and will likely be somewhat familiar with your organization. But mission and vision statements are written for the "person on the street," someone not familiar with your organization, as well as employees. In this sense, both are designed to tell a general reader something about your organization. Both are designed to inspire and motivate organizational members, not through the kind of clichéd language you might find on those "motivational" posters, but through providing a destination and way to reach that destination. Finally, while perhaps broad in scope, both are clear and unambiguous.

There are certainly differences as well. Quite simply, a vision statement is a description of where you and your organization want to be at a given time in the future (what you want to accomplish, how you want to evolve) and a mission statement is a description of *how* you and your organization intend to achieve your vision. In short, the vision statement addresses the future and the mission statement focuses on the present. The vision statement is timeless in the sense that it addresses realistic, attainable, yet far-reaching goals. For example, Amnesty International's vision, taken from its website, is:

> of a world in which every person – regardless of race, religion, ethnicity, sexual orientation or gender identity – enjoys all of the human rights enshrined in the Universal Declaration of Human Rights (UDHR) and other internationally recognized human rights standards.
>
> *(Amnesty International 2015)*

The popular home store IKEA's vision is even simpler: "To create a better everyday life for the many people" (IKEA 2012). What these statements have in common is that they are written to give a general reader information about the company as well as to inspire its employees and remind them of the organization's vision.

Notice that each statement is fairly broad and focuses on something in the future which may never be fully realized. Will everyone eventually enjoy all of the human rights mentioned in Amnesty International's vision statement? A pessimist may say no, but it's something toward which they have vowed to strive. IKEA wishes to "create a better life" for everyone. What does that mean? It's pretty broad, but it's a vision statement and it's supposed to be broad. Nonetheless, each gives readers an idea of what that organization is all about.

A mission statement is a bit narrower and focuses on goals, purposes, and primary objectives. Nike's mission statement is: "To bring inspiration and innovation to every athlete* in the world" (Nike 2015a). According to Nike's website, the asterisk refers to "The legendary University of Oregon track and field coach, and Nike co-founder, Bill Bowerman [who] said, 'If you have a body, you are an athlete'" (Nike 2015b). Notice that with Nike's mission statement we're more specific, even down to the particular type of customer: athletes. Similarly, Amazon.com's mission is "to be Earth's most customer-centric company, where customers can find and discover anything they might want to buy online, and endeavors to offer its customers the lowest possible prices" (Amazon.com). Again, note the specificity with which the organization sets out its mission. The mission of each company is clearly set forth for readers inside and outside the organization.

While some self-help literature suggests that a single person should write vision and mission statements for him or herself to motivate and inspire him or herself, the vision and mission statements above are written for a fairly broad audience. Policy, vision, and mission statements are less personal (unless you're the founder or CEO, perhaps) than other types of writing you may do outside the classroom. Below, I cover a few more professional types of writing: e-mails, reports, memos, and blogs/websites.

E-mails

As a teacher for over 20 years, I've seen a lot of changes in the ways students communicate with their professors. While e-mail was once the great new invention that facilitated communication between students and professors, it now seems that many students find it an antiquated and old-fashioned way to communicate. I have answered students' questions via tweet and Facebook (I have both a Twitter account and group Facebook pages for class), but I still prefer e-mails. For many students, however, the only time they use e-mail is to communicate with professors and certain companies' customer service representatives (and even the latter is now often done through real-time online chats). Nonetheless, writing e-mails is still a common "real-world" writing practice. This section isn't about business and professional writing per se, but I am compelled to offer some tips and relate them to what I've covered so far (see the box "Writing Professional E-mails").

First, just like policy and mission statements, being clear and concise is key. And just as with policy and mission statements, you must consider your audience when writing e-mails. While people may enjoy reading policy and mission statements (the latter, at least), many people *do not* like reading e-mail. The clearer and more to the point you can be, the better (Purdue Owl 2010).

Writing Professional E-mails

1) Include a relevant and descriptive subject line
2) Indicate the reason for sending the e-mail in the first couple lines.
3) Indicate a proposed plan of action or expected outcome if relevant.
4) Avoid humor or jokes, as they don't often translate to e-mail.

The common factor in writing for your classes and some types of writing you may do in your professional career is clear: you must consider your audience. While a consideration of audience is just one of the three components of the "Tao of Writing," topic and occasion being the other two, you must think about your audience in relation to *everything* you write. This may seem obvious, but think back to all the papers you've written. How often do you get "into your own head" and write things that seem to make sense to you without considering how others may read them? Granted, stepping outside of ourselves, getting out of our heads, and reading what we've written from another's perspective is difficult. But it's the first step to being a good writer, whether we're writing papers for a class, mission statements for our company, or e-mails to a fellow employee.

Reports and memos

Reports and memos are two types of professional writing common in the workplace, especially for people in management and leadership positions. Both have much in common with the types of writing we've already discussed. For example, job website Monster.com explains that good reports and memos have a *clear purpose*, a *consideration of audience by anticipating readers' questions*, and a *clear focus* (Lester 2016). It's important to remember that a report shouldn't read like an academic research report you might write for one of your classes. However, there are similarities. You need to hook the reader by providing a concrete description of the problem, event, or issue that prompted you to write it in the first place. And as with mission statements, you will often be called upon to include specific goals or recommendations for readers (inside the company and/or outside the company) based on your assessment of said problem, event, or issue. Further, you will have to provide specific ways for your readers to enact and realize those goals or recommendations.

Memos differ from reports, as memos are shorter, not as detailed, and usually meant for an internal audience (inside the company). Respected writing website Purdue Owl (Perkins and Brizee 2010) lays out the content for successful memos:

- An *opening segment* gives readers the purpose of the memo (reminding employees of a dress code, for example), the context of the problem (some people not following the code), and a specific assignment or task (remember to follow the dress code, or employees should speak to a manager if they feel they are unable to follow the guidelines).
- A *discussion segment* includes details to support the ideas laid out in the opening segment. If a memo is longer than a page, a *summary segment* may be necessary to give readers concrete takeaways.
- Finally, a *closing segment* politely reminds readers of the actions you want them to take.

Blogs and website copy

Perhaps the most common type of professional writing done these days, blogs and website copy share many qualities with reports and memos. And as with reports and memos, it's important to keep in mind the three components of the TAO of writing: topic, audience, and occasion. First, you obviously must know about your topic. Whether it's a product, an issue, a service, or something else, do your research (Kuik 2013). Doing your research can help you visualize your ideal reader or audience. Once you can describe your ideal reader as you might be able to describe a friend, you can imagine yourself having a conversation with this reader (Duistermaat 2013). This will help you fashion a readable writing style, something essential for website copy. When imagining a conversation with your ideal reader, you can't forget about the reason for the conversation in the first place. *Why* are you having this conversation? What's the occasion? Unlike a normal conversation, chances are you want the reader to buy something (product or service) or *buy into* something (an idea or opinion, for example). As such, you will want to entice them, hook them, and get them to read on.

Chances are, though, your audience won't want to read too much or for too long. Imagine the difficulty maintaining readers' attention when they have so many other online options that might prompt them to click away from your site (social media, their favorite sports site, etc.). So, keep the sentences and paragraphs short, and use lists. This will ensure your readers get what they need in the quickest and clearest manner possible. As with reports and memos, you will need to be clear and concise for your online readers.

Chapter Summary

In this chapter we've covered some basics of writing. We've framed some common assumptions about writing academic papers in an attempt to gain the proper mindset for writing such papers. In the process, we've debunked some myths about writing. While you might be writing your papers by yourself (unless you instructor lets you co-author with another student), it's important to ltlok.yoeo

remember that you're not alone in your journey. As cheesy as it may sound, you're entering a *community* of people – other student, amateur, and professional writers – from whom you can draw knowledge, wisdom, and "tricks of the trade."

One thing we can learn from people who've been doing this for a while is that there are *no shortcuts*. But, there's also no great mystery to it. As you may have gleaned from the famous writers quoted in this chapter, the old adages about work are indeed true. To paraphrase two of these sayings: half of writing is just showing up; and writing is 1% inspiration and 99% perspiration. In short, writing isn't a mystical process where the words suddenly come to you from some ethereal place. Writing is, for the most part, organizing your ideas, thinking about your audience, and putting one word after the other. In short, *connecting* to your topic and *connecting* your thoughts to each other will help you *connect* to your readers.

Finally, this chapter has covered the types of papers you might be expected to write in your classes, the types of writing you might be expected to do once you leave the classroom for a professional career, and how the writing skills you learn in your classes are eminently transferable to virtually any career you might enter. The next chapter gets down to basics regarding class papers, beginning with brainstorming and moving to a more in-depth consideration of audience.

References

Amazon.com. No date. "About amazon.com Facebook Page." Accessed July 20, 2015 from https://www.facebook.com/Amazon/info?tab=page_info.

Amnesty International. 2015. "Our Mission." Accessed September 5, 2014 from http://www.amnestyusa.org/about-us/our-mission.

Burrell, Gibson, and Morgan, Gareth. 1979. *Sociological Paradigms and Organizational Analysis: Elements of the Sociology of Corporate Life*. London: Heinemann.

Carroll, Lewis. 1920. *Alice's Adventures in Wonderland*. London: Macmillan.

Craig, Robert T. 1999. "Communication Theory as a Field." *Communication Theory*, 9: 119–161. DOI: 10.1111/j.1468-2885.1999.tb00355

Duistermaat, Henneke. 2013. "Six Simple Steps to Writing Seductive Web Copy." Last modified June 27, 2013. Accessed March 12, 2016 from http://www.copyblogger.com/seductive-web-copy/.

Eatherington, Mel. 2015. "Employees Lack Writing Skills in the Workplace." Accessed July 19, 2015 from http://www.wcu.edu/academics/campus-academic-resources/writing-center/employees-lack-writing-skills-in-the-workplace.asp.

Eisenberg, Eric M., Goodall, Harold L., and Trethewey, Angela. 2014. *Organizational Communication: Balancing Creativity and Constraint* (7th ed.). New York: Bedford/St. Martin's.

Gaiman, Neil. 2014. "Ten Rules for Writing Fiction." *The Guardian*, February 19, 2010. Accessed July 19, 2014 from https://www.theguardian.com/books/2010/feb/20/ten-rules-for-writing-fiction-part-one.

Gellman, Andrew and Basbøll, Thomas. 2013. "To Throw Away Data: Plagiarism as a Statistical Crime." *American Scientist*, 101: 168–171.

IKEA. 2012. "Our Business Idea." Accessed September 5, 2014 from http://www.ikea.com/ms/en_IE/about_ikea/the_ikea_way/our_business_idea/index.html

Kiuk, Kyra. 2013. "How to Write Effective Copy for Your Website." Last modified May 2, 2013. Accessed March 12, 2016 from https://www.distilled.net/blog/distilled/content/how-to-kick-ass-at-copywriting-for-your-website/.

Kuhn, Thomas. 1962. *The Structure of Scientific Revolutions*. Chicago: University of Chicago Press.

Lester, Margot Carmichael. 2016. "How to Write Better Reports and Memos." Accessed March 12, 2016 from http://www.monster.com/career-advice/article/how-to-write-better-reports-and-mem.

Merrigan, Gerianne, and Huston, Carole L. 2015. *Communication Research Methods*. New York: Oxford University Press.

Messmer, Max. 2012. *Human Resources Kit For Dummies* (3rd ed.). Hoboken, NJ: John Wiley & Sons.

Miller, Henry. 1964. *Henry Miller on Writing*. New York: New Directions.

Nike. 2015a. "About: Our Mission." Accessed September 5, 2014 from http://about.nike.com/.

Nike. 2015b. "Get Help." Accessed September 5, 2014 from http://help-en-us.nike.com/app/answers/detail/a_id/113/~/nike-mission-statement.

O'Farrell, Renee. 2015. "The Importance of Good Writing Skills in the Workplace." *The Houston Chronicle*. Accessed July 19, 2015 from http://smallbusiness.chron.com/importance-good-writing-skills-workplace-10931.html.

Pacanowsky, Michael, and O'Donnell-Trujillo, Nick. 1983. "Organizational Communication as Cultural Performance." *Communication Monographs*, 50: 127–147. DOI: 10.1080/03637758309390158

Perkins, Courtnay, and Brizee, Allen. 2010. "Parts of a Memo." Last modified September 24, 2010. Accessed November 6, 2016 from https://owl.english.purdue.edu/owl/resource/590/02/.

Purdue Owl. 2010. "E-Mail Etiquette." Last modified April 17, 2010. Accessed November 6, 2016 from https://owl.english.purdue.edu/owl/resource/636/01/.

Weick, Karl. 1995. *Sensemaking in Organizations*. Thousand Oaks, CA: Sage.

UC-Davis (University of California-Davis Administrative Policy Office). "Guide to Writing and Maintaining Campuswide Administrative Policy." Accessed February 20, 2015 from http://manuals.ucdavis.edu/resources/Guideto WritingPolicy.pdf.

Further Reading

Check out the website "Brain Pickings" for more advice from established writers: http://www.brainpickings.org/index.php/2013/05/03/advice-on-writing/.

Stephen King's book *On Writing: A Memoir of the Craft*, although dealing with his fiction writing, still has some great advice for the practice and work of writing.

2

Brainstorm and Research: Formulating and Answering Questions

Chapter Learning Outcomes

- Distinguish among several types of brainstorming techniques
- Analyze audiences of written scholarly work

Composing Research, Communicating Results: Writing the Communication Research Paper,
First Edition. Kurt Lindemann.
© 2018 John Wiley & Sons, Inc. Published 2018 by John Wiley & Sons, Inc.

- Pose research questions that lead to enhanced understanding of topics
- Apply effective outlining strategies
- Identify techniques for effective research into scholarly literature

Chapter Features

- "Write Away"
- Building Blocks
- Engaging Ethics

Imagine you're in class and your teacher is explaining your paper assignment. She says, "The topic can be anything that strikes your interest, whatever you want to write about." What is your first reaction on reading that sentence? Panic? Relief? Even more than actually putting words to paper, the toughest task for many students is to answer the question, "What should I write about?" Instructions like "Write about whatever you want" can be a welcome refrain for students who like the wide-ranging freedom to write about whatever they like (as long as it's related to the class, of course). For others, however, those words can incite instant mental paralysis, creating a spiral of questions and doubts. Whatever your reaction to these words, this chapter is designed to help you brainstorm and organize ideas for your paper.

The Purpose of This Chapter

One of the most crucial phases of writing a paper doesn't involve reading, writing, editing, or research; it involves coming up with an idea for your paper. Indeed, generating a paper topic and research on that topic can be the most daunting task for students. Certainly, talking a topic idea through with your instructor can be a helpful process. But there are things you can do on your own to spark ideas, fan the flames once that spark catches fire, and tame and refine your fire into a controlled burn. You might commonly know this process as *brainstorming*. As the Writing Center at the University of North Carolina (2012) explains, brainstorming allows you to "take advantage of your natural thinking processes by gathering your brain's energies into a 'storm'" (para. 2). This chapter offers you some tools to help you successfully complete one of the most important parts of writing the paper: the brainstorming and research process.

Brainstorming Topics: What Are You Interested In?

One of the most important questions to ask yourself when beginning a paper assignment is: What are you interested in? You should choose a topic that will sustain your interest (University of Illinois 2015), and *not* just something for which you think you can easily find sources. *Brainstorming* is the method by which you might touch on an idea that will sustain your interest. The writing process for any paper should begin with brainstorming. As the name implies, the beginning part of this process should be a *storm of ideas* coming quickly. Imagine yourself out in a rainstorm, except instead of water it is raining scraps of paper on which are written certain phrases and words related to your topic. You're collecting them in a bucket. The rain stops, and you look down in the bucket. There are a lot of ideas in there, for sure. Luckily, there's more to brainstorming than just collecting ideas. You begin sorting and evaluating them, deciding what to toss and what to keep.

This approach, while seemingly simple, presents problems for many students. The most common problem is that students might evaluate ideas too early in the process. In this age of immediate gratification, one-click shopping, and same-day shipping, some students get ahead of themselves and want the perfect topic immediately. But the evaluation of ideas is the second step in the brainstorming process. Imagine trying to sort the ideas as they fall from the sky before you've even collected them all! Of course, ideas don't rain down from the sky; we have to invent them. The following section is meant to provide you with some idea-generating techniques, some ways to begin to *collect* ideas.

Idea mapping

Sometimes called "mind mapping" (Mindmapping.com), idea mapping is a way to generate concepts related to your main topic and visualize connections between them. This works best on a sheet of paper, but we'll cover some other non-paper options below. For now, the first step is to write your topic or area of interest in a sentence or phrase in the middle of a blank sheet of paper and circle it. It should be in the middle of the page, according to the inventor of mind mapping, Tony Buzan (2011), because your brain then has the freedom to branch out in any direction that occurs to you. While Buzan incorporates images and color coding into his techniques, just focus on words and phrases to keep it simple.

After writing the word or phrase that best represents your initial topic idea, ask yourself, "What does that phrase make me think of?" Quickly write that word or phrase in another circle and draw a line from it to your original topic or area of interest. Then repeat the process, except now you can connect to either your main topic or area of interest, or the second bubble or circle that branches off from your initial word or phrase. Continue doing this for any word or phrase that inspires you. As you proceed, don't worry about how closely or tangentially connected you are to your initial topic area. You'll have a chance to sort through all these circles later. The first part of idea mapping is to just write down whatever you think of, being careful not to censor yourself.

Let's take a look at a hypothetical example for a real class that is often taught in communication departments: interpersonal communication. Let's imagine our paper assignment is to write about a contemporary issue facing college students' interpersonal relationships. While interpersonal relationships could include friendships, let's pretend we're going to write a review of scholarly literature on romantic relationships. We might write "romantic relationships" in the center of our page. That might make us think of sex, so we write that in a circle and draw a line. Now, we can branch off of "sex" or our original "romantic relationships." We may think of sexually transmitted diseases when we read the word "sex," so we write it, and draw a circle and a line to the word "sex." Now we have three words to

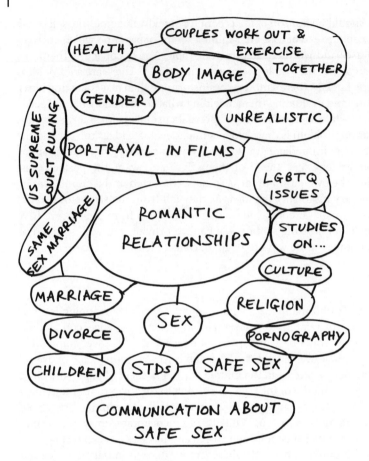

Figure 2.1 Idea-mapping: example

consider. STDs may make us think of "safe sex," so we repeat the process. And so on. When we're done, we end up with a page that looks something like Figure 2.1.

Notice that we suddenly have a lot of options for a paper that originally had "romantic relationships" as its very broad – too broad, in fact – topic. If we were to conduct research on our original topic of romantic relationships, we would no doubt find a multitude of scholarly sources from a number of fields ranging from communication to psychology to sociology and everything in between. But with idea mapping, we can effectively narrow our topic to: the relationship between exercise and relationship satisfaction; the effect of romantic films on perceptions of romance among couples; the meanings of marriage to same-sex romantic couples; the role of religion among romantic couples; and the list goes on and on.

Going through this process, you'll likely end up with a page full of words. But this is just the first stage. Table 2.1 offers a breakdown of all the steps involved in the idea-mapping process.

Let's return to the idea-mapping example. Our initial topic of romantic relationships now includes a consideration of safe sex and on-campus education, as well as religious views about premarital sex. If we were to continue our idea

Table 2.1 Idea-mapping guidelines

---

1) Write your topic idea in a sentence or phrase in the middle of a piece of paper and draw a circle around it.
2) Write the first thing you think of when reading your topic. Draw a circle around that word or phrase and connect it to your main topic.
3) Read both your original topic and your second word or phrase. Write the first thing either makes you think of. Draw a circle around the third word or phrase and connect it to the relevant word or phrase.
4) Repeat until your page is filled.
5) Go to the circles on the outermost edges of your page. Does anything you've written sound like a topic in which you might be interested? If so, great, you've got a topic. Repeat this process for that topic.
6) If nothing sounds like it might be a viable topic on its own, begin to trace the circles closer to the center of the paper, where your original topic idea is written.
7) If nothing sounds like a workable topic, return to your original idea in the center of the page and reverse the process, examining the circles from the center of the page outward. Chances are, many of the words or phrases written in the outer circles are sub points for your main topic and areas in which you might need to provide evidence.

---

mapping onto another page, cohabitation (living together, something becoming more common among college students), might also enter the picture, as might concepts like secrecy and self-disclosure. Suddenly, our initial idea, which was admittedly broad and unwieldy for a paper, has morphed into a more focused topic: communication about sex. When we begin to do library research on this topic, we'll be able to spend less time sifting through journal articles that are about various aspects of romantic relationships unrelated to our topic of communication about sex. We'll go into more detail about library research later in this chapter. But let's first review some other approaches to brainstorming.

Write Away

Choose a topic you're currently working on. Try idea mapping with it. Don't stop creating word circles until you've completely filled the page. Following the idea-mapping guidelines in Table 2.1, choose a topic word or phrase that is narrower than your original idea; this could come from a circle branching off your original idea branching off a related word.

Take this new word or phrase and do another session of idea mapping. Once you've filled the new page with word circles, choose three you think could be your main points. Do a quick library database search and see what you come up with. Is there enough on your main points? If not, choose different ones. See the outlining guidelines later in this chapter for tips on creating an outline.

Using mobile devices. Not surprisingly, there are many different apps for our phones and tablets that allow us to do idea or mind mapping without ever writing anything down by hand. The list of apps is numerous, including many free ones. You can find an initial breakdown of some of the best ones here: http://www.pcworld.com/article/226084/mobile_mindmapping_apps.html. If you're an Android user, check out this comprehensive summary of available mind-mapping apps: http://xslab.com/2014/02/10-great-mind-mapping-apps-for-android/.

Freewriting and journaling

While idea mapping is a way to brainstorm in relatively short bursts, freewriting and journaling are more long-form approaches. These can be used in conjunction with idea mapping or in place of it. Freewriting and journaling, however, should not take the place of writing actual drafts of your paper.

Freewriting

Similar to the notion of drafting a paper, freewriting adopts the perspective that we may not know what we think about a topic until we write about it. It is designed to "free your mind" and unlock potential thoughts, opinions, feelings, and related topics. It accomplishes this through a sustained, uncensored writing period that may cover anything from your personal feelings to how you're feeling about the freewriting experience itself (e.g., "I hate this. I don't know what to write about..."). Natalie Goldberg (1986), author of the famous how-to book *Writing Down the Bones*, explains that in this exercise you should keep your hand moving, don't cross out anything or worry about spelling, and don't think rationally (as in, "What does this have to do with my topic?"). That said, if you begin with an intention of exploring your thoughts on a topic, chances are, something you write will be relevant.

Although Goldberg's exercise is useful to get us putting pen to paper, you might be working with a deadline when trying to brainstorm for a paper assignment. So, when freewriting to explore a particular topic, it's important to maintain some rules and guidelines to keep as focused as possible: see Table 2.2.

If you've done this early in your paper-writing process (for example, as soon as you get the assignment from the instructor), you can set it aside for a few days and look at it later. When you do read it over, you should scan it for ideas about your topic. You may find new ways of thinking about your topic, points and sub-points for an argument, or perhaps even a new topic.

Journaling

Journaling is another useful brainstorming technique. Journaling isn't just good for brainstorming; it's been found to increase cultural sensitivity (Schuessler, Wilder, and Byrd 2012), reduce stress and process negative experiences (Lyubomirsky, Sousa, and Dickerhoof 2006), and assist in the learning process,

Table 2.2 Freewriting guidelines

---

1) Write the topic or idea at the top of the paper.
2) Write whatever comes into your mind. Don't worry about whether what you're writing is relevant to your paper or topic; you'll be able to go back and read it through later.
3) Set a period of time during which you will do nothing but freewriting, for example 10–15 minutes.
4) Keep writing during this time period. Even if you have to write about your feelings about writing, don't let yourself stop.
5) Don't worry about grammar or spelling; you're not writing your actual paper, so those don't matter during freewriting.

Table 2.3 Journaling guidelines

- While sporadic journaling is good to provide entry points into a topic, it can also be used in a sustained manner when working on a semester-long project (or a longer one, such as a thesis).
- Journaling can be done electronically or written by hand. The most important thing is for the process to be convenient for you.
- Journaling is most useful when regularly scheduled.
- Journaling is for you and you only. You need not pressure yourself to come up with a masterpiece when journaling.

Table 2.4 Additional brainstorming techniques

- **Fill in the blank**. Complete the following sentence: My topic is about _____. Chances are, the more words it takes you to complete the sentence, the less formed your topic is. While you don't want an extremely broad topic, you want to be able to complete the sentence in the most specific way possible, with the fewest words possible.
- **Abstracts**. Write a paragraph that summarizes your entire paper, from beginning to end, including your conclusions. Use it as a map for your paper. If your paper changes direction, no problem. Just rewrite your abstract and keep going.
- **Elevator speech**. Imagine your teacher will grade you solely on the basis of what you can explain to him or her at a conversational pace (not talking fast) on an elevator ride (choose the number of floors you will travel, but not a skyscraper with 100 floors, or that would defeat the purpose of this exercise!). You have to be concise and clear, to the point yet sufficiently scholarly.

especially in adult learners (Brady and Sky 2003). The benefits are numerous because it calls on writers to reflect on their experiences and critically analyze them. So, while idea mapping and freewriting are designed around a goal – for example, to brainstorm on a particular topic or idea – journaling is often less goal-directed but more constructed. Unlike freewriting, in which you try to write continuously for a certain period of time, with journaling you can take as much or as little time as you like. You also may formulate complete sentences and put more effort into carefully crafted sentences. There are some guidelines to keep in mind for journaling depending on what you want to get out of the experience: see Table 2.3.

There are other less time-intensive ways to brainstorm for your topic. Below, I cover a few that have worked for me with my own writing.

Other brainstorming techniques

Like the brainstorming strategies covered above, these other options (Table 2.4) aren't meant to take the place of outlining, which we'll cover later in this chapter. These are just additional techniques that might help get you thinking about a paper topic; each approach is meant to be used in conjunction with the more in-depth brainstorming methods detailed earlier in the chapter.

Fill in the blanks

Finish the following sentence: "My paper is about _____." Can you fill in the blank with one word? Two? Chances are, the longer it takes you to complete this sentence, the less formed and the vaguer your thesis and, eventually, your paper will be. Sometimes it's useful to try to put your idea in a succinct, structured sentence and "see how it sounds" to you.

Abstracts

Abstracts are more involved than a fill-in-the-blank exercise but are nonetheless useful in helping you get your thoughts together. Similar to the paragraphs you might read at the beginning of published scholarly articles that summarize the article, abstracts are meant to provide the reader with a short summary of your paper: why a reader needs to read it, what others have written about that topic, what theories you have used in writing about this topic, and what the reader will learn by the end of your paper. Not all class papers will require abstracts, but this may be a useful exercise nonetheless.

Elevator speeches

The middle ground between the fill-in-the-blank exercise and the abstract is the "elevator speech." This exercise asks you to imagine you're in an elevator with a person of importance who has the power to fund your research or, in this case, grade your paper *only on the basis of what you can tell them during an elevator ride*. For example, imagine your teacher will be grading you only on what you can tell your teacher in the time it takes you to get to your desired floor. Consider the characteristics such a speech must contain. It has to be succinct, to the point, and easy to understand. Trying to put your paper idea into such a format can help you formulate thoughts and arguments.

The brainstorming techniques covered in this chapter so far provide a multitude of different approaches to getting your topic ideas down on paper and shaping them in ways that audiences (readers) might begin to understand. And if you notice, a common thread in the last three brainstorming techniques is *audience*. Thinking about your audience (I will use "audience" and "readers" interchangeably from here on out) is important in all stages of writing your paper, even the brainstorming stage. We're going to pick up this thread and continue thinking about audience as we work our way toward conducting research on a topic.

Now That You've Got Your Topic: Thinking about Your Audience

Coming up with a topic is tricky. The first trick is finding something that interests you. The second trick is coming up with a topic that interests your audience. We've already covered the most difficult part: getting an idea that will sustain your interest for the duration of the paper-writing process. We're now going to address the second trick: thinking about what the audience already knows and wants to know about your topic (Figure 2.2). This is easier than the first step

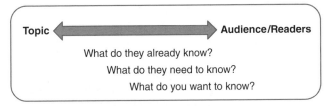

Figure 2.2 Arrow spanning the topic and audience with questions

(finding a topic we like) because we can be sneaky about it: there are ways we can *make* our audience care about our topic (or get them to think they *should* care).

Asking questions and answering those questions with research is part of creating a bridge between you and your topic, and the audience. There are two important questions you must ask your audience, which we explore below.

What do they already know?

What does your audience already know about your topic? Well, that depends on who your audience is, doesn't it? So, to answer this question, you first have to think about the audience: your readers. Unless your instructor is very specific about whom you're writing for, there will likely be three audiences for your class papers: your classmates, your instructor, and a general audience of interested readers with base-level knowledge of your topic. I offer some considerations of each below.

Your classmates
Depending on how your instructor has set up the writing and drafting process, your classmates may be reading drafts or the final version of your paper. Regardless, it's a good idea to assume your classmates are part of the audience for your paper. They have roughly the same level of knowledge as you do, and while you may know more about your topic than they do because of all the research you did (or will do) for your paper, you can also assume they possess a basic knowledge about the content covered in your class.

Your instructor
Your instructor, who is also in the audience for your paper, probably knows more than you do about the topic. Maybe not. Often, when I teach my research methods classes to undergraduate and graduate students, they know more about a particular topic because they've done extensive research on it for the entire term. If your instructor is like me, then he or she will not be grading you on whether you're *smarter* than him or her. In fact, your instructor probably wants you to teach him or her something new in your paper. Nonetheless, it's also safe to assume your instructor has base-level knowledge about the content as it pertains to your class.

A general audience
So, it's relatively easy to get a grasp on the first two types of audiences. Your classmates and your instructor are in the class with you and have probably been exposed to roughly the same content as you. More difficult to integrate

into your paper preparation is an assessment of what the general audience *outside* of your class already knows about your topic. These outside readers aren't necessarily lay people (people outside of your classroom, school, and academe), but those in your field or discipline but *not* in your class. Translating research to a general audience is a useful endeavor in which many scholars are engaging (Giles 2008; Goodall 2000; Tracy 2013). Unless your teacher explicitly instructs you to write for a lay audience, consider this general audience to be readers who still enjoy (or don't mind) reading research papers with scholarly citations. Certainly, they may not know about specific theories, but your class-mates might not either; you're presumably doing research on a specific area with which your classmates may be unfamiliar. In each case, then, you'll prob-ably have to explain your concepts in a "break it down" moment, laying out the general tenets or applicable parts of the thing you're studying and the theories or concepts you're applying.

Anticipating what your audience already knows will help you fast forward to more important parts of your paper and skip the things you think your reader already knows. For example, you may be writing a paper about conflict among romantic couples. While your classmates and instructor may be familiar with how conflict is conceptualized in the interpersonal communication literature, a general audience may not. Therefore, you may need to define and explain what you mean by "conflict." Conversely, you may be writing a paper about communi-cation in civil demonstrations and protests. Will you need to describe and explain how such protests played a prominent role in ending U.S. involvement in Vietnam in the 1970s? If your general audience is a U.S. audience, you probably won't need to go into too much detail about that. However, if your general audience is pre-dominantly from another country, you might have to. Likewise, you may want to include a consideration of the history of free speech and protests and want to mention "Speakers' Corner." What is that? If you're from the United States you may not know, but those in Great Britain likely know it is a famous free speech spot in Hyde Park in London (http://www.speakerscorner.net/). So, if your audi-ence is British, you may not need to explain this; U.S. audiences may require some details.

Ultimately, it's up to you to anticipate what your readers may already know about your topic. But dividing up your audience into three categories should help you immensely. What you can assume is that your classmates and instructor have a basic knowledge of your concepts, but that a general audience may need some additional explanation of particularly complex theories or concepts. Before you think these explanations will be a waste of time and paper, keep in mind that explaining these to a general audience will not only make your paper more acces-sible, but it will also illustrate to your instructor that you have a working knowl-edge of class content.

What do they need to know?

What your audience already knows, or what you can assume they know, is quite different than what you think they might *need* to know about your content. You might be writing a review of literature about homeless individuals and how they communicate with those from housed society. Your audience may not know a whole lot about homelessness, but you probably want to argue that they *need* to know about the problem of homelessness. You might do this by citing statistics that point to an increase in homelessness in major U.S. cities (Green 2013; Palta 2015). I used a similar argument in my research on homeless newspaper vendors in San Francisco, arguing that this phenomenon might be an increasingly common sight in major cities if the U.S. economy continued to falter (this was back in the late 2000s) (Lindemann 2007). I knew I had to find a reason for readers in other parts of the country and world to care about this (unfortunately, homeless people selling specialized newspapers is a common sight in other major cities across the globe). Regardless, in cases like these, you'll be informing readers *and* persuading them to care about your topic and to read your paper.

As you may have gathered, what an audience already knows and what they need to know about a particular topic will likely be two different things. What you think they *need* to know, they may not yet know. This requires both informing and persuading them. In both cases, you must put yourself in your readers' place and imagine you're reading your own paper. This is a skill that will be useful when you actually begin writing and editing your paper. But if you're still in the brainstorming phase, why do you need to anticipate what your audience already knows and needs to know about your topic? For the same reason you need to consider what *you* want to know about the topic: *the answers will determine what you research*. We will cover the process of researching later in this chapter. And we still have more questions to ask ourselves.

Asking Questions: What Do You Want Know?

Let's set aside our audience of readers for a moment. We can't lose sight of what might have started us down this road. In case you forgot, it was *your* interest in the topic. So, ask yourself one more question: What do *I* want to know about my topic? Although you may have many factual questions about your topic (dates, numbers, statistics, etc.), you can categorize the types of questions you might ask under three headings: theoretical, practical, and research questions.

Theoretical questions

What does something mean? This is a question that falls into the category of theoretical questions. Kurt Lewin wrote in 1951 that "there's nothing so practical as a good theory" (169). And while I do believe that's true, my use of the term "theoretical" here is meant to separate the academic from the "real world" (that distinction is one that may not be totally accurate, but it is necessary for the purposes of our discussion here). By "theoretical questions," I mean asking questions about your topic that are more abstract and scholarly.

For example, you might be writing about disability and communication. As you think about the communication field and disability, you might wonder how other scholars have written about disability. There are theoretical issues involved in your question, which may simply boil down to: "How does the research conceptualize disability as communicatively co-constructed?" Formulating a response to this question will require you to examine the scholarly journals and closely read them for a theoretical and, admittedly, somewhat abstract sense of the relationship between communication and disability. This question, of course, has implications for the ways people actually communicate with others with a disability, and how people communicate about disability; but, at its core, this question is what we would call a theoretical question.

Theoretical questions aren't the only important questions to ask when devising a research plan for your paper. Most scholars would vehemently disagree with the idea that their work exists solely in the abstract realm with no practical applications. So, asking questions that are applicable to the world outside your classroom is another important part of your research plan.

Practical questions

Theory is important. In fact, we all have theories about how the world works, whether it's the best way to get a parking spot on campus, the quickest way to get to work in the morning, or even how to go about preparing meals. In this sense, theories are "practical." For academic research papers, however, different people may have different ideas of what is practical. What is considered applicable by a physicist, for instance, will differ from what is considered practical by a sociologist. By "practical questions," I simply mean questions that don't involve theory. In short, the *actual language* of your practical question shouldn't involve a theoretical concept (such as "communicative co-construction," in the theoretical question in the previous section). Going back to our example of disability and communication, you might ask practical questions like, "How does family communication change when a family member is physically disabled from an injury?" You might also ask, "What are the media stereotypes of people with disabilities?" The language for these questions is concrete and specific, and avoids abstract terms.

You may or may not find a direct answer to practical questions in the scholarly literature, but you can imagine that a whole host of keywords that might arise from such questions that would help you with a database search (something we'll address later in this chapter). Asking theoretical and practical questions, whether you are conducting research for a literature review, an original data-based paper, or any other kind of class assignment, will help you generate keywords and a direction for your research. But how does one *ask* a question? That deceptively simple query is covered in the next section.

Types of research questions

You might be wondering, "Didn't we just cover types of research questions?" Well, yes, sort of. We covered the *kinds*, or large categories of questions. Theoretical and practical questions are useful considerations in beginning your paper-writing process. But when we consider specific *types* of questions we can get a better sense of exactly *what* we want to know and *why*. It is useful to ask questions with a specific *intention*, which will help you get a better sense of the purpose of your paper.

Questions of understanding

Questions of understanding are some of the most useful for guiding literature reviews and qualitative research projects that involve textual or rhetorical analysis, or another kind of "close reading" of a text. These questions don't necessarily look for correlations or precise relationships between variables. Instead, they pose broader inquiries into the nature of a phenomenon. These questions might be called *interpretive*, as they can often be found in qualitative research that's interpretive in nature (Merrigan and Huston 2015; Tracy 2013). This type of question is useful to point you in your research toward a broad sense of *how* something works.

Let's say your topic is the communication of grief in families after a loved one has passed away. You might ask a variety of practical questions, like: "How do families communicate about the illness of a loved one?" or "What family communication occurs when a loved one has passed away?" You might also ask theoretical questions of understanding, including: "How does the communication literature describe family communication in the context of grief?" and "How has social science studied grief and communication?" In each case, you want to know *how* communication functions in family members' connections with each other in the wake of a loved one's passing.

Overall, questions of understanding seek a broad understanding of a particular topic or phenomenon. Questions of understanding are most often used in qualitative and rhetorical studies and in guiding literature reviews. While the question may imply an effect of one thing on another, like grief on family communication, questions of understanding do not seek to *measure* that effect; these questions simply help to discover *how*.

Questions of effect

When conducting original data-driven research that includes designing and administering questionnaires, surveys, or experiments, questions of effect often prove more useful than questions of understanding. While you will likely encounter *hypotheses* in a quantitative study, i.e., statements that predict that one variable will affect another (perhaps in a particular way), such studies may also pose research questions about the impact of one thing on another. Literature reviews may also pose questions of effect by proposing hypotheses without actually testing the variables. Specific questions of effect can also lead you down a particular path in your research into scholarly literature.

Let's return to our example of grief and family communication and consider a new, practical, question: "What effect does grief have on family communication?" This question can be answered in a couple of ways, depending on the type of study being done. A researcher might answer this question by securing a sample population and administering a survey. Since this isn't a methods textbook, we won't delve into the details of that sort of study (you can check out Allen, Titsworth, and Hunt 2009; Merrigan and Huston 2015; and any number of quantitative methods books for more on conducting a quantitative research study). Fortunately for us, questions of effect apply to conducting a literature review as well.

By asking a question of effect before conducting our search for sources, we will be led to certain types of answers. We can cull the various studies performed on the topic and present to the reader a few answers based on a categorization of the findings. In short, we might conclude that, based on a review of the literature, "grief seems to affect family communication in the following ways …" and then present those ways to the reader. As with questions of understanding, we're getting at the *how* of something; the difference is that here we're presenting some variables or relationships to the reader.

Questions of action

Questions of understanding and effect are certainly similar to each other. Questions of action differ in that such questions lead the author to recommend, or suggest that the reader adopt, a particular stance, attitude, or belief. These questions might be most commonly associated with critical rhetorical or qualitative research (Merrigan and Huston 2015; Tracy 2013). Obviously, then, the paper that results from asking what kind of action *should* be taken will probably be more persuasive in nature than the paper we might get from asking the first two types of questions. However, these papers may not always be explicitly telling the reader "You should do this!" Returning to our hypothetical topic of grief and family communication, we might ask a practical question like, "What are the most effective ways family members can communicate grief over the passing of a loved one?" The sources and subsequent organization of our paper this question might lead us to wouldn't necessarily be along the lines of "You should do this," but more like "Research has shown these to be the most effective communication strategies." Implied is the idea that readers would be advised to use these communication techniques should the need ever arise.

As you can see, questions of understanding, effect, and action can be theoretical or practical in nature. The important thing to remember with these types of questions is that by asking them, we will be led down a particular path in our search for supporting sources. Granted, we may draw on the same sources for multiple types of questions, but the question we ask will prompt us to *read* those sources differently and *take away* different things to put in our own papers.

Finding Research: Who Knows about This Topic and What Do They Know?

But how do we find those sources? Should we just Google them? While that's probably what most of us would do initially, it's not necessarily the best place to start. Too often, students simply search for sources using a jumble of keywords and get overwhelmed. More focused searching will make the whole process smoother and less intimidating. In the following sections, we'll cover how to conduct a more focused search for sources.

Using keyword searches

Keywords are the words and phrases we enter into whatever database or search engine we're using to find our sources. But where do these keywords come from? You might be tempted to simply write a list of keywords associated with your topic, but if you've been following this chapter closely, you've already done this work. Remember the brainstorming techniques we covered earlier in this chapter? We're going to revisit those techniques to generate some keyword searches.

Building Blocks: Generating Keywords

Take a look at any of the documents you created from your brainstorming session(s). These could be idea-mapping sheets, freewriting, journal entries, abstracts, or even your elevator speech. With any or all of these documents, complete the following steps:

1) Cross out all the conjunctions (and, the, a, an, etc.).
2) Cross out all the modifiers (very, like, etc.).
3) Circle the first ten nouns that catch your attention.
4) Use these nouns in various combinations in the search engines you use to find sources for your paper.

Using keywords to research sources takes creativity. Sometimes, entering the exact word or words for your topic may not yield much. When this happens, relax; this can actually be a good thing! Why? Because it means you're forging new territory with a truly original topic. For example, let's say you want to study the communication of masculinity among vegetarian men (men who don't eat meat). A Google search might reveal some websites and online magazine stories. A search of your library's database may reveal only a few scholarly journal articles. But you're supposed to include 15–20 sources for your research paper! This is a time when you might go to your instructor's office and tell her you can't find enough sources. Before you do that, though, you should try thinking about your topic from a different angle.

A different way to approach your keyword search is surprisingly simple: back up a little. In the case of your hypothetical topic above, you might simply search for "masculinity" and "vegetarianism" separately. You might also search terms like "gender," "diet," and "health" and see what comes up. At any rate, remember: don't let the sources you find (or don't find) dictate how you write your paper.

Don't let the sources you find (or don't find) dictate *how* you write your paper. It's your argument, not someone else's.

Of course, you shouldn't make up sources, nor should you claim a source says something it doesn't. But getting creative means finding sources that may not say exactly what you want them to, but can still be used as evidence and support. Think of it this way: a brick is not a house, but it helps to build one. Likewise, a source – whether it's a book, a scholarly article, an online magazine story, a government report – is not your paper. A source is merely one of the bricks you use to build your paper.

Engaging Ethics

As difficult as it is to find sources for your paper, it can be tempting to "cut corners." This might mean making up sources, but for most students it means one of two things. The first and most common ethical pitfall students face is intentional or unintentional plagiarism. We'll address plagiarism in more detail in Chapter 3. For now, let's address the second most common pitfall, citing secondary sources. Secondary sources are sources cited by another author or authors that you want to cite. For instance, any of the sources I've cited in this chapter are considered, for you, secondary sources. Sometimes, you might like what another author has cited and, to pad the number of citations for your paper, you cite all the sources that the author you're reading has cited. According the American Psychological Association (APA), whose citation style you might be required to follow for a class paper (and which we cover in Chapter 3), secondary sources should be cited *only* if that original source is out of print, not written in your native language, or otherwise unavailable (APA 2015).

A sure way your teacher might figure out you're citing secondary sources is when you cite a quotation from an author in which he or she cites a number of sources. For example, let's say the following sentence appears in a paper:

> Moore (2015) notes many problems with past studies, explaining that "Smith (2013) claims that the study of relationships conducted by Jones (2010; 2012) and Martin (2009) are flawed" (194).

What in the world is going on here? Well, the student author is quoting Moore directly, and the sentence he is quoting just happens to cite an article by Smith, who in turn cites two studies by Jones and one study by Martin. Already we have a problematic direct quotation, as this student author can – and *should* – easily paraphrase Moore. But, let's say this student includes the citations by Smith, Jones, and Martin in his References page, and this direct quotation is the only place in which the Smith, Jones, and Martin articles are cited in the paper. This student has just committed plagiarism by communicating to the reader that he's read these sources when, in fact, he hasn't; Moore has. In essence, this student is misrepresenting Moore's work as his own.

If this all sounds pretty complicated, you're right. Fortunately, there's a sure way to avoid this. *Always* try to read and cite the original source.

Sometimes, you might get lucky and hit on the right combination of keywords immediately. Whether it takes a long time or a short time to find your sources, you may have to do a little thinking about the combination of keywords. By going back to your brainstorming techniques, you should have the tools necessary to conduct a thorough search for sources.

Communication and social science databases

You've got your brainstorming documents, and you've generated keywords for a search. What's next? A search engine like Google is probably your first thought. While that has its advantages (and disadvantages), let's start with your

Table 2.5 Common databases for finding scholarly sources

- **Academic Search Premier**. Includes articles, magazines, and newspaper articles on all subjects.
- **Communication and Mass Media Complete**. Communication and mass communication-related articles, as well as entries from encyclopedias and handbooks.
- **ERIC**. Three databases (EBSCO, Firstsearch, and ProQuest) offer everything from journal articles to dissertations, ranging from science to the humanities.
- **MLA International Bibliography**. Some of the same sources as in EBSCO, but even more humanities-oriented articles and documents.
- **Project MUSE Journals**. Journals from university presses in the humanities and social sciences.
- **Sociological Abstracts**. Journals, books, book chapters, dissertations, and more in sociology and related disciplines.

---

own school's databases. Many college and university libraries have online databases on which you can find a variety of sources. Table 2.5 lays out several of these options from a multitude of possible databases. Be sure and check your own school's library site for complete options.

Starting with any of your library's databases is better than going straight to a Web search engine, for a variety of reasons. First, you know what you're getting. If you were to use Yahoo or Bing, for example, and enter search terms, you might see government documents and trade publications (magazines) in addition to journal articles. If your teacher specifies only journal articles for your references, that could be a problem for you and your grade. Second, many databases offer full texts (depending on your library's subscription), which will allow you actually to read the sources you're citing. You may not get full texts with other search engines.

Using the Web: Reminders

Let's say you do a library search but still want to use the Web. You might be looking for scholarly sources, or you might be looking websites. In fact, you may not know what you're looking for, only that you need sources. Hopefully, your searches aren't that scattershot, and you're searching *intentionally* using the types of theoretical and practical questions covered earlier in this chapter. But, perhaps you're anxious to get going on your paper and you figure, "What's the harm in just seeing what's out there?" Certainly, there's no harm in checking. But before you begin thinking about which sources you might want to use, there are some important things to keep in mind, detailed in Table 2.6.

There are some other useful sites to check out as well. Google Scholar can be a treasure trove of potentially useful source citations. When getting journal articles from Google Scholar, though, just cite them as you would a print source; this is ethical, will make life easier for you, and will cause less confusion for readers. We cover the commonly used citation styles in Chapter 3.

Table 2.6 Guidelines for using Internet sources

- Know what you're looking at. What kind of site is this? Who's the author? What are their credentials? If it's not evident from the site itself, Google them to find out. Remember, by citing this source you're telling the reader to trust this source.
- Try to stick to sites that end in .gov or .org. These are governmental or organizational sites and can often be counted on to have reliable, verified, and up-to-date information. They are usually viewed by readers as more credible than the usual .com sites.
- Look for the last updated date on the site. This ensures that your own research is as current as possible. Additionally, including this information in your reference makes your research look more thorough and complete.
- Note the paragraph when making a direct quotation. While you should always try to paraphrase, include the paragraph number when quoting directly.

Outlining

Once you have a topic and a substantial number of sources, you're ready to begin organizing your paper. While you may not know exactly what your argument is yet, you can begin to think about it on paper. Outlining provides a perfect opportunity not only to organize your thoughts, but also to do some additional brainstorming. Sometimes instructors require outlines from students; in this case, you might have certain rules you must follow, such as using complete sentences in your outline. If not and you're outlining only for your own benefit, then you have the freedom to outline whatever way you like.

Regardless, there are some guidelines that will help you get the most out of your outlining process. The first is the rule of *subordination*. This simply means that your Roman numeral headings are more general than your letter headings, which are themselves more general than the Arabic numeral sub points, and so on. In short, the top heading should always be more general than the points under it. For example, if I were outlining this particular section of this book, it might look like this:

I) Outlining
   a) Rules for Outlining
      1) Subordination

Notice that the heading "outlining" is the most general of these headings, and the further in from the margin, the more specific each point is. This will help you organize your thoughts by keeping track of your main points and your sub points.

The second guideline for outlining is *division*. This simply means that you should have more than one sub point for any main point. The reasoning behind this can be summed up by thinking about the very word the rule is named after: division. If you divide an apple, you have two halves. The apple is your main point, and the two halves are your sub point. Certainly, you could cut the apple into three or more pieces, but you will have at least two pieces when you cut. You cannot divide an apple and have only one piece. In this way, then, you cannot divide your main point and have only one sub point. You must have at least two

Table 2.7 Rules for outlining

- **Subordination.** Make sure your sub points are more specific in the information and description than the headings above them.
- **Division.** When creating sub points for a main point, always have at least two.
- **Parallel wording.** Make sure each heading reads the same way and that all use the same part of a sentence (e.g., pronouns, verbs)
- **Coordination.** Each point should have the same degree of significance as the other headings of the same level. In short, if your main points are Roman numerals, you should not use Roman numeral for a sub point.

sub points. If we revisit the sample outline for this section, then, it seems we need to add another sub point:

I) Outlining
    a) Rules for Outlining
        1) Subordination
        2) Division

Of course, the rule of division means you also have to have a point B to go along with point A in the previous example. In this case, point B could include any topic related to outlining, as long as it wasn't a rule of outlining. When you follow the rules of subordination and division, you are assured a fairly detailed outline. There are a few other rules that help you even further. Another useful guideline is *parallel wording*. This guideline helps us to fashion our points in a similar manner. For example, if one of your Roman-numeral points is a pronoun, the other ones should be as well. The table of contents at the beginning of this chapter follows this rule. Consider the main headings, with Roman numerals added:

I) Brainstorming Topics
II) Thinking About Your Audience
III) Asking Questions
IV) Finding Research
V) Outlining

Notice that each heading is a verb: brainstorming, thinking, asking, finding, outlining. The parallel wording helped me remember that each main heading details a *process*. For each section, then, I was reminded that I needed to adopt a "how-to" approach in explaining things. This rule works well with another rule called *coordination* (Purdue Owl 2013), which means you should ensure each of your headings has the same degree of significance. When you use parallel language, you can similarly keep track of your main points. Table 2.7 offers a reminder of these outlining rules.

Chapter Summary

This chapter has covered a lot of what is called the prewriting or invention stage of writing a research paper. The first section covered, brainstorming, offered some tips on creating topics and setting you up to search for sources. And while a topic that will sustain your interest should be your first goal for a research paper, your second goal should be fashioning a paper your audience is interested in. To this end, this chapter also provided some questions to ask to get you thinking about your audience, something many students fail to do. The next section laid out some tips and guidelines for conducting research, both in your own library's databases and on the Web. Finally, remembering some simple rules for outlining will help you get your thoughts together to begin writing your paper. The last section of this chapter was designed to help you do just that.

All this may seem like a lot of work, especially when you can just sit down at your computer and begin typing away. But that approach may not result in a well-written paper (or a good grade), and all this prewriting work will pay off when you actually begin putting one sentence after the other. Before that, though, we have one more thing to consider: constructing arguments and providing support for those arguments. I address this important part of the process in Chapter 3.

References

Allen, Mike, Titsworth, Scott, and Hunt, Steven K. 2009. *Quantitative Research in Communication*. Thousand Oaks, CA: Sage.

APA (American Psychological Association). 2015. "How Do You Cite a Source That You Found in Another Source?" Accessed October 30, 2014 from http://www.apastyle.org/learn/faqs/cite-another-source.aspx.

Brady, E. Michael, and Sky, Harry Z. 2003. "Journal Writing Among Older Learners." *Educational Gerontology*, 29: 151–164. DOI: 10.108003601270390157006

Buzan, Tony. 2011. "7 Steps to Making a Mind Map." Accessed September 26, 2014 from http://www.tonybuzan.com/about/mind-mapping/.

Giles, Howard. 2008. "Accommodating Translational Research." *Journal of Applied Communication*, 36: 121–127. DOI: 10.1080/00909880801922870

Goldberg, Natalie. 1986. *Writing Down the Bones*. Boston, MA: Shambala Publications.

Goodall, H. L., Jr. 2000. *Writing Qualitative Inquiry: Self, Stories, and Academic Life*. Walnut Creek, CA: Left Coast Press.

Green, Emma. "Homelessness Is Up in New York City, but It's Down Everywhere Else." *The Atlantic*, December 13, 2013. Accessed October 24, 2014 from http://www.theatlantic.com/business/archive/2013/12/homelessness-is-up-in-new-york-city-but-its-down-everywhere-else/282315/.

Lewin, Kurt. 1951. *Field Theory in Social Science: Selected Theoretical Papers*. Edited by Dorwin Cartwright. New York: Harper & Row.

Lindemann, Kurt. 2007. "A Tough Sell: Stigma as Souvenir in the Contested Performances of San Francisco's Homeless Street Sheet Vendors." *Text and Performance Quarterly*, 27: 41–57. DOI: 10.1080/10462930601046012

Lyubomirsky, Sonja, Sousa, Lone, and Dickerhoof, Rene. 2006. "The Costs and Benefits of Writing, Talking, and Thinking about Life's Triumphs and Defeats."

Journal of Personality & Social Psychology, 90: 692–708. DOI: 10.1037/0022-3514.90.4.692

Merrigan, Gerianne, and Huston, Carole L. 2015. *Communication Research Methods*. New York: Oxford University Press.

Mindmapping.com. 2015. "Theory Behind Mind Maps." Accessed September 25, 2014 from http://www.mindmapping.com/theory-behind-mind-maps.php.

Palta, Rina. 2015. "Officials: Homelessness Jumps 12 percent in Los Angeles County." Los Angeles, CA: KPCC, May 11, 2015. Accessed November 30, 2016 from http://www.scpr.org/news/2015/05/11/51616/homelessness-increasing-in-los-angeles-according-t/

Purdue Owl. 2013. "Four Main Components for Effective Outlines." Last modified March 1, 2013. Accessed November 9, 2016 from https://owl.english.purdue.edu/owl/resource/544/01/.

Schuessler, Jenny B., Wilder, Barbara, and Byrd, Linda W. 2012. "Reflective Journaling and Development of Cultural Humility in Students." *Nursing Education Perspectives*, 33: 96–99. DOI: 10.5480/1536-5026-33.2.96

"Speakers' Corner." Accessed October 26, 2014 from http://www.speakerscorner.net/.

Tracy, Sarah. 2013. *Qualitative Research Methods: Collecting Evidence, Crafting Analysis, Communicating Impact*. Boston, MA: Wiley-Blackwell.

University of Illinois Library. 2015. "Choose a Topic." Last modified July 22, 2015. Accessed November 6, 2016 from http://www.library.illinois.edu/ugl/howdoi/topic.html.

Writing Center, University of North Carolina at Chapel Hill. 2012. "Brainstorming." Accessed July 26, 2015 from http://writingcenter.unc.edu/handouts/brainstorming/.

Further Reading

For more on brainstorming techniques, check out the "Mind Tools" page at http://www.mindtools.com/brainstm.html.

3

Making Arguments, Providing Support

Composing Research, Communicating Results: Writing the Communication Research Paper,
First Edition. Kurt Lindemann.
© 2018 John Wiley & Sons, Inc. Published 2018 by John Wiley & Sons, Inc.

Chapter Learning Outcomes

- Identify the argument in any paper
- Distinguish the types of claims made in an argument
- Identify warrants in your and in other arguments
- Distinguish among the most common types of research citation styles
- Identify common citation mistakes that lead to plagiarism

Chapter Features

- Student Spotlight
- "Write Away"
- Engaging Ethics

How many times have you recommended a movie, a television show, or some music to someone, only to have that person give you a lukewarm reception? Did you persist and try to convince them to see that movie or listen to that song? If you engaged in this common topic of conversation, you just participated in argument-making. Indeed, making arguments is something we do on an almost daily basis (some may even say that most communication is persuasive in nature). Nonetheless, when faced with making an argument in a class paper, many students react as if making arguments were as difficult as a learning a new language. While argumentation is, perhaps, a different language, it's one you already know.

The Purpose of This Chapter

In this chapter, we'll explore the important parts of understanding and creating arguments, including supporting arguments with evidence and properly citing that evidence. One of the ways we'll do this is by finding connections between what you already know and some theories of argumentation you may not yet know. We'll also go over some common citation styles you might be asked to use in your papers. Rather than simply telling you to cite this way or that way, I'll try to break down each of the three styles with easily understandable *reasons* for the requirements of each style.

Every Paper Is an Argument

Just as some communication scholars believe that nearly all instances of communication are persuasive (Cialdini 2007; Stiff and Mongeau 2003), I'd like you to think about every paper you write as an argument. What does this mean? It will mean different things depending on the specific assignment, but in the simplest terms: whenever you write a paper, imagine you're trying to convince the reader of something. Sometimes, this may only be in the introduction to a paper, in which you must convince the reader that your topic is important enough and relevant enough to the reader's life for that person to *keep reading*. Other times, this might mean that you're trying to convince readers to believe something, adopt a particular point of view, or simply strengthen their existing beliefs, values, or attitudes. In either case, the reader must at least be interested enough to keep reading. And you can generate this interest by thinking about your papers as arguments.

What are we talking about when we say "argument"? There are several conceptions of argument and argumentation, ranging from Greek philosophers like Aristotle to more contemporary feminist communication scholars (Foss and Griffin 1995; Griffin 2011). For the purposes of this chapter, I'll be using persuasion and argument in conjunction, with persuasion being the desired end result of an argument. Aristotle viewed both as part of the rhetorical process, which he described as recognizing the available means of persuasion in any situation (time, place, relevant topics, and audience) (Bitzer 1968; Kennedy 1991). For communication scholars Sonja K. Foss and Cindy Griffin (1995), persuasion happens in a more communal fashion in which a speaker or author invites the audience into a dialogue. Through dialogue, the speaker and audience (or author and reader) might collaboratively construct a perspective on which they both agree.

Writing for an audience is and is not like this last example. While you certainly want to invite the reader into your world and engage the reader in a dialogue, readers' attention spans (like public presentation audiences' attention spans) are notoriously short and getting shorter (Goleman 2013; Watson 2015). Sometimes, there's not enough time or available space to ease into such a relationship. Sometimes, you have to meet audiences where they are, in their world, in their lives, and tell them why they should keep reading. Granted, knowing if this is happening with the reader while he or she is reading your paper is impossible; unlike public speaking, you don't get immediate feedback from your audience. Nonetheless, the more closely you hold the reader in your mind when writing, the stronger the relationship between you and the reader is likely to be.

Importantly, this view of the reader is consistent with our discussion in Chapter 2. This idea departs from the commonly held notion that, since your teacher is the primary reader, he or she *has* to read your paper. They do, of course, but the danger is in thinking you don't have worry about keeping their attention. This attitude won't transfer well to the world outside the classroom walls. Out in the "real world," as those in academe (teachers and students) sometimes call it, people *don't have* to read your writing, whether it's an e-mail, a memo, a blog, or a magazine article. If they're not interested, or if they feel it doesn't apply to them, they very well may stop reading! So, convincing the reader to keep reading is a large part of creating writing that people *want* to read. The last part of Chapter 1 explicitly focused on some examples of non-classroom writing, but let's face it, you're probably most concerned with writing your class assignments. So, below, we'll cover mainly classroom writing. But you can apply these concepts to many other types of writing as well.

You have something important to say!

A common concern I encounter from students is that they feel they don't have anything to argue, at least in an academic context. Sometimes, they can't find a topic they feel passionate about. I especially hear this with paper assignments in which students can pick from virtually any class-related topic out there (and that's a pretty vast area to choose from). While students may not mean to say that they just don't care about anything, that is, in fact, one message they're communicating to me: "I don't care about anything, therefore I can't find a topic I like despite the freedom to choose anything in the world to write about." I don't believe that's true, of course. And when students come to me with this problem, I recommend that they do some brainstorming (see Chapter 2 for a review of brainstorming techniques). I also try to reframe their approach to the assignment: sometimes the term "argument" makes us think we must be an expert about a particular topic. I tell these students, that's what research is for – you don't have to be an expert on a topic to *want* to write about a topic, but chances are, you will be an expert *after* you've done the research and written the paper.

With this in mind, let's get a few things out of the way as we start. First, as I explained at the beginning of the chapter, making an argument is something we do every day. We know how to make *those* arguments, whether they involve borrowing something from a friend or convincing someone to go to a particular restaurant. But when the argument becomes "academic" in a classroom setting, we often assume some other set of skills is involved. Sure, research is involved. However, the process is still the same: we believe something, and we try to convince others to believe it, or at least *consider* believing it. Second, writing an argument doesn't mean the topic has to be life-or-death. Often, students think that, since they're supposed to be arguing something, the topic should be earth-shattering, life-changing, and *serious*. While topics like bullying and coming out are certainly worthy of making some kind of argument about, other topics – like sibling communication or social media use – aren't any less worthy. We just have to first convince our audience of readers that what we have to say is important enough for them to pay attention.

"But why," you might ask, "should the audience pay attention to what I think? It's just my opinion." Well, besides all the research that you will do on this topic, making you in all likelihood more educated on the topic than most of your audience (your classmates), this type of paper is about making and supporting an argument. Is that argument your opinion? Yes and no.

Fact or opinion? Both!

As a university professor who teaches classes that involve a lot of writing, I get this question a lot: "Is this paper supposed to be fact, or my opinion?" You can probably guess my answer from the title of this section: It's both! In fact (pardon the pun), most of the class papers you write that require you to do some kind of library research and synthesize that research into a coherent paper will be a combination of fact and opinion. The "facts" in these kinds of papers are the articles and information you locate and cite in your paper, although those articles are themselves arguments made by other scholars. The "opinion" part of these papers is, of course, the argument you make. These two work together. You make the argument, and you use the "facts" of others to support your argument.

But is there a difference between opinion and argument? In the context of classroom writing, definitely. While I use the two interchangeably in this chapter, I don't mean you should view them as one and the same. We hear the term "opinion" and we usually think of a personal preference or belief about something. Hopefully, our opinions about something are informed by research. Maybe someone has an opinion on the Middle East conflict, and this opinion is informed by research, reading newspaper articles, watching the news, or maybe even personal experience. But if you think back to friendly disagreements you might have had with someone, you may remember hearing, "Well, that's just my opinion." Meaning, "That's what I think, and you may disagree, but you can't tell me I'm wrong because it's my *personal* opinion." That's not what we're talking about in this chapter when we talk about argument.

I'd like you to think of argument and opinion as intertwined. Fowler and Aaron (2011) explain that the main assertion of an argument is always an opinion. In this vein, our working definition of argument is simply *a set of statements constructed to work together in order to attempt to convince a reader to accept the terms, premise, propositions, and ideas of the author as plausible, reasonable, and worth thinking about.* There are few important facets of this definition that will help structure our discussion in the rest of this chapter and what we will cover in Chapter 4, like claims, reasons, and warrants. I provide an overview of those aspects in the following sections.

Every argument needs support

While our opinions expressed in daily interactions may be based on extensive research, they usually aren't. Sometimes our opinions are based on an imprecise and incomplete synthesis of various things we've heard, seen, and experienced. Not so with arguments, at least with your class papers. The support for your arguments in your class papers will come from research articles and credible news sources. That said, some students think their arguments are limited to the research that exists about a particular topic. Not so. Your arguments, while grounded in research, are your own; in that sense, the arguments are only limited by your ability to find sources.

In other words, an argument shouldn't be organized around evidence. *Evidence should be organized to support the argument.* And there is a difference. In the former case, we might think we are only allowed to argue things for which evidence already exists. Let's say you want to argue that superhero movies make a profound social commentary on attitudes toward those who are viewed as different (outside the traditional norms) by mainstream society. That sounds like an interesting argument. Has anyone else out there said this? Possibly. But what if you don't find anything? Does that mean you shouldn't write about the topic? Of course not. It just means you need to return to your brainstorming documents and generate some more keywords for searches. When you do, you may find that you can make that argument by citing as evidence studies on intercultural communication, behavior viewed as "deviant" by mainstream society, and research on the acceptance of LGBTQ individuals and people with disabilities. While these aren't superpowers heroes may possess in the movies, these people may similarly be viewed as "different" from others on the basis of their race, religion, ethnicity, body, and sexual orientation.

In short, you need to *make the evidence work for you*. You have something important to say. Don't be afraid to say it just because you think no one else has.

The Toulmin Method

Although we're familiar with arguments from our everyday communication inter-actions, making an argument in an academic paper can be more difficult than it sounds. To help us understand this process better, we're going to turn to a famous model of argumentation known for both its broad applicability and its simplicity: the Toulmin Method is an oft-cited, tried and true framework for thinking about *how* arguments work and how to *write* an argument. If you search "Toulmin Method" online, you'll likely find slightly different labels for each part of an argu-ment (Purdue Owl 2014). However, the main parts are generally all the same and consist of: a *claim* (sometimes *qualified*), *grounds* or *evidence*, and the *warrant*. Usually, you'll also find *backing* and often *rebuttal* (Toulmin 2003). We're going to go through each of the parts of an argument, examining how actual students have used them in their papers. An overview is offered in Table 3.1.

Making claims

The first and most important part of an argument is the claim. This is the thesis statement of your argument. In fact, it can often function as the thesis statement of your paper, providing a framework for the rest of the paper. A popular website for paper composition questions and tips, the Purdue Owl (2014), defines a claim as "The overall thesis the writer will argue for" (para. 3). For example, an analysis of the British film *Love, Actually* (Curtis 2003) might include the claim, "This film presents an insightful, albeit unrealistic, examination of the different stages of romantic relationships." Obviously, there's more to this argument, as it requires support in the form of evidence (scenes from the film, quotes from reviews, etc.), but if the paper assignment asked you to apply relational communication con-cepts to a film, this sentence might work as a claim.

Table 3.1 Overview of parts of an argument

Parts of an argument	Function
Claim	The thesis of the argument; the main point, expressed in a sentence.
Grounds or evidence	Support for the claim: can be statistics, examples (hypothetical and real), and testimony from experts, among other things.
Warrant	The often unspoken statement of reasoning that connects the claim and the evidence.

Additionally, claims are not always blanket statements, but can include *qualifiers.* In this particular example, the words "albeit" and "unrealistic" are qualifiers to the claim. Consistent with what we discussed earlier in the chapter, this claim is the basis for an original argument you are making, not necessarily something already stated in a published argument. Therefore, you may also find support in the form of scholarly articles about relationships or any of the issues the film addresses, like cross-cultural communication, grief, and infidelity.

While a thesis statement can be thought of as the "point" or "gist" of your paper, a claim is a bit more complex. Not only can there be qualifiers, as we just discussed, but your claim can also be thought of as a particular type of claim. Below, I cover three different types of claims that you might use in any given paper assignment: claims of fact, value, and policy (Toulmin 2003).

Claims of fact

First, let's discuss what "fact" means in this context. Making a *claim of fact* doesn't mean you necessarily have to argue for something that exists as a universally accepted truth, one you might find written down somewhere. Indeed, if you were just stating a fact, for example that the Earth's radius is 3,959 miles or 6,371 km, it wouldn't really be an argument as no reasonable person could disagree with it. This statement has been scientifically proven. So, claims of fact aren't statements of proven scientific principles.

In a paper written for one of my classes, two first-year MA students, Jose and Jeff, made a claim of fact in their original research project, a study of tabletop role-playing games (TRPG) like Dungeons and Dragons. The claim was: "Communication and trust are not only essential to the TRPG experience, but they make up the TRPG experience." Now, is this a fact in the sense that the Earth's radius is a fact? Of course not. Rather, it's a statement that a particular situation or relationship commonly exists with TRPGs. The authors eventually prove this about relationships through observations of role-playing games and interviews with participants.

It's important to note that claims of fact aren't the sole province of empirical data-driven research. Claims of fact can also be made with literature reviews and other types of library-research papers. For example, a student conducting a literature review on conflict in group communication and relationships might make the claim that "Studies of conflict in groups *usually* propose collaboration as the most desirable method of conflict management, but *rarely* offer concrete ways in which such collaboration might be accomplished." Note the qualifiers in italics. In this case, the author is arguing that this particular situation or state of affairs exists in the context of scholarly literature on group conflict.

Claims of fact, then, don't treat facts as something that is already scientifically proven, like the radius of the Earth or the properties of an element or chemical compound. Instead, claims of fact propose that a situation or state of affairs exists. This situation or state of affairs (the current state of some aspect of life, relationships, organizations, population, community, etc.) could be a relationship between variables that will be studied by means of a data-driven research project (which might be proven with a *social science* method), or it could be an argument that scholarly research on a particular topic doesn't address some aspect of that topic completely. Either way, these claims grow out of an author's informed opinion on a subject, one that he or she will attempt to argue for in a paper.

Claims of value

While claims of fact propose that a state of affairs exists, *claims of value* propose that a current situation, artifact, or state of affairs is good, bad, positive, negative, helpful, harmful, or somewhere in between. As with claims of fact, someone making such a claim would seek to *prove* a claim of value. But unlike a claim of fact, a claim of value will not use the evidence to prove a situation, relationship, or state of affairs *exists*. Instead, someone making a claim of value will use evidence to illustrate why this particular situation, relationship, or state of affairs not only exists, but is desirable, undesirable, or somewhere in between. In short, claims of value employ a value judgment to *critically* assess the relative properties of a topic, artifact, or situation.

Claims of value, then, are often employed in a critical analysis. Some topics and paper assignments appropriate for such a claim might be persuasive in nature, like "The communication climate of politics in the United States is devoid of logic, reason, and compassion." A student making such a claim would still seek to prove this claim but would understand that she is doing so from a critical perspective. Like claims of fact, these types of claims are also an author's opinion, but are perhaps more obviously an opinion like one you might hear in daily interactions (such as a movie recommendation). Regardless, making a claim of value also entails providing evidence to support it, something we will cover later in this chapter.

Claims of policy

The term "policy" probably conjures up images of a government think tank or lawmakers deliberating on state or federal laws. This may be the case with some such claims, which may argue that a particular law should be changed or repealed. In class paper assignments, however, these claims can also appeal to readers on a personal level by persuading them to alter or strengthen their current attitudes or beliefs. In short, *claims of policy* are applied arguments designed to better society in some way. Claims of policy combine aspects of the previous two claims. Like claims of fact, they posit that some current situation exists. Like claims of value, they argue that this current situation is good, bad, positive, negative, desirable, or undesirable. Claims of policy differ, however, in that they argue that the audience should move in a certain direction, be it attitudinally or behaviorally.

As you might guess, claims of policy aren't often employed in empirical data-driven studies conducted in a social science vein, where some form of objectivity is desired. Making such a claim would require a suspension of the presumed objectivity that usually accompanies scientific studies. While such research may be prompted by the desire to study something the researchers consider a problem, the conventions of traditional social science writing usually discourage an explicit statement of opinion. Instead, claims of policy are often used in rhetorical analyses of artifacts (speeches, films, images, etc.).

Table 3.2 Types of claims

Claim	Function
Fact	To argue (and prove) that a situation or state affairs exists.
Value	To argue (and prove) not only that a situation or state of affairs exists, but that this situation is desirable, undesirable, good, bad, etc.
Policy	To argue (and prove) that a situation or state affairs: exists, is good, bad, etc., *and* should be acted upon by readers in some way (attitude change to behavior change).

Surprisingly, though, claims of policy can also be used in library-based research papers. Consider this claim of policy from one of my undergraduate organizational communication students: "Since we cannot avoid dealing with power and its distribution throughout society, it is important that we critically examine power to see how people strategically accumulate and disseminate power within organizational structures." This paper explored the ways power is conceptualized in organizational communication, but it's clear that the claim means to persuade readers that a critical examination is good or desirable. This critical examination is the policy – or action – about which the author is attempting to persuade readers. Table 3.2 lays out the differences between the types of claims we've discussed.

Ultimately, the claim you make in your paper depends on your topic and the parameters of the assignment for which you're writing. But whatever claim you make, you will have to *support* your claim. The Toulmin Model (Toulmin 2003) for understanding and analyzing arguments explains that there are multiple ways to support claims. The next sections are devoted to helping you understand how you might support your claim.

Providing backing and evidence for the claim

Arguments aren't something we just make for a paper. Whether it's convincing someone to go see a particular movie, trying to borrow a car from a roommate or family member, or attempting to get an instructor to accept a late paper, arguments are a part of our daily lives (although hopefully you're not trying to convince your teacher to accept late papers on a daily basis!). In the course of making these arguments, we employ claims. And if our claims are to be convincing in any way, we must use *backing* and *evidence* (Toulmin 2003) to support our claims. While both backing and evidence can be used to support our claims, the purpose or focus of each is different. The *backing* for a claim is broad, such as supporting statements and propositions, while the *evidence* for a claim is more specific and micro-level, such as testimony, statistics, and concrete and examples. We'll cover the differences in the next section.

Backing

As noted above, backing can be thought of as supporting statements for your claim. Just like claims, we use these statements, which can also be called the *reasons* for our claim, in our everyday arguments. Consider a fairly ordinary, everyday movie recommendation. We might say to a friend, "You should go see this movie while it's still playing in the theater." Our friend might trust us and go see the film, no questions asked. But going to the movies can be expensive nowadays. So, maybe our friend needs more to go on besides our recommendation. A logical response from him might be, "Why?" As in, "Why should I go see this movie?" If we simply say, "Because it's really good," that may not be enough to convince our friend. So, we might tell him that a certain actor is in the film, or that it has a lot of fast-paced action, or that it's funny. Each of these reasons can be considered backing for our original claim; they are supporting statements, statements that support our claim. Obviously, we might need to offer *evidence* to "prove" these statements, but we'll get to that later in the chapter. For now, think about the papers you might be asked to write for class in a similar way to this movie recommendation example.

Let's go back to a claim a student might make if she were assigned to apply interpersonal communication concepts or models to a film. Remember that our running example for this chapter is a paper is analyzing the classic British romantic comedy *Love, Actually* (Curtis 2003). Her claim is: "This film presents an insightful, albeit unrealistic, examination of the different stages of romantic relationships." What might our backing be for this claim? Well, it certainly depends on the student's argument, but some examples of backing statements could be:

1) This film portrays multiple relationships involving a diverse population: age, race, class, occupation, and degree of commitment.
2) This film portrays some of the negative, as well as positive, aspects of relationships, including unrequited love, conflict, and cultural barriers.

These statements are the backing for this student's claim, the *reasons* for her claim that the film, while unrealistic, provides insight into different stages of romantic relationships.

As you might imagine, each statement of backing could potentially become a section of the paper and a mini-thesis for that particular section. But this student's work is not done. Obviously, she needs to support these statements with *evidence*, which in turn will support her claim. For this hypothetical paper, the evidence she will provide could include descriptions of certain scenes in the film, dialogue from characters, and quoted reviews of the film from "experts" (reviewers for websites, newspapers, and magazines), all of which are framed with the interpersonal communication concepts she is using to analyze the film.

There are many different kinds of evidence that can be used to support a claim, and I have only mentioned a few above. It's important to note that each type of evidence has its own advantages and disadvantages. I go over some of the main types of evidence, as well as when you might use each, in the next section.

Using evidence

Put simply, evidence is used to support a claim. More specifically, evidence is what you use to "prove" your statements of backing, or reasons for the claim. There's a reason why I've broken down the structure of an argument in this way. It's easy to get overwhelmed if you think about all the ways you could and should support your claim. Thinking only about providing support for your backing statements will put the entire argument in a more comprehensible format, and a more manageable one when you actually begin to write your paper.

For example, in our hypothetical example of a paper applying interpersonal communication concepts to the film *Love Actually*, one statement of backing is "This film portrays multiple relationships involving a diverse population: age, race, class, occupation, and degree of commitment." Think about what you might expect in the way of examples for this statement if you were a reader of the paper. You would probably expect to read a little about at least one relationship in the film that might have age as a factor (there is a junior high school student who likes one of his classmates), race as a factor (an English-speaking man is in love with a woman from another country who speaks very little English), class and occupation as factors (one prominent politician has feelings for a woman from a working-class family), and degree of commitment as a factor (the film follows conflict in a couple who have been married for many years).

Would this student have thought to describe each of these relationships if she were to just try to prove her claim that this film presents an insightful, albeit unrealistic, examination of the different stages of romantic relationships? Maybe, but she might also get overwhelmed with the possibilities. Providing statements of backing allows her to then focus on particular examples as evidence. And these examples are one type of evidence she could provide. The next section covers the different types of evidence you might consider in supporting your backing statements.

Types of evidence

When I teach public speaking classes, I always take care to tell students that statistics aren't the only type of evidence that is persuasive. I do this because I began to notice over the years that students often provided statistics where an example (a story or anecdote from a researched source, for instance) would be just as, if not more, compelling. Statistics wouldn't work as compelling evidence with our hypothetical class paper on the film *Love Actually*; statistics about the box office gross of the film would do little to prove it's an insightful examination of relationships, nor would numbers about how many people saw it in the theaters or afterwards on video. So, it's important to understand the multiple kinds of evidence you might provide as support or backing, as your topic and argument may require you to provide different types of evidence. *Statistics* are certainly one acceptable type of evidence, but statistics provide a broad snapshot of a certain aspect of the phenomenon, a bird's-eye view of the issue. And statistics can't zoom in to put a human face or emotional appeal to the issue you're examining.

Examples, which would likely work in this hypothetical film analysis paper, can come in various forms. I'm using a hypothetical example (a paper on the film *Love Actually*) to illustrate my point about the use of examples. But examples can also be real, taken from newspaper or magazine stories. Because examples often contain descriptive and sometimes emotionally charged language that tells a short story about something, examples can go a long way toward helping the reader see, smell, hear, and feel the experience about which you're writing.

Testimony, quotations or words from other people, are another kind of evidence. When doing a review of literature, you might use other authors' words.

If these authors hold a credible position regarding your topic, for example a scientist or professor who studies the topic, their words can be considered *expert testimony*. Certainly, words from others not considered "experts" can still be compelling. For instance, a paper about the media effects of advertisements on perceptions of body image might include the following claim: "Advertisements that portray body types consistent with traditional femininity promote unrealistic perceptions of gender." In this paper, you might find quotations from girls who relate what they think of these advertisements. While these quotations may not be "expert" in the sense of coming from a researcher or professor, they nonetheless may provide powerful backing for your claim.

Understanding that statistics aren't always the most compelling type of evidence and that testimony can be just as if not more powerful in terms of supporting a claim is just half the work of using evidence in a paper. Knowing what kind of evidence to use is much different than knowing how to incorporate evidence into a paper. The question then arises: How should you work this testimony into your claim? I provide some suggestions and tips in the next section.

Quotation or paraphrase?   How do you work testimony into your paper? An all too common way is to directly quote (while properly citing the source, of course). Unfortunately, this way of using testimony, expert or otherwise, can be the least effective and compelling. Granted, reading the words of someone else, especially if those words are crafted in an artistic, poetic, poignant, or otherwise unique way, can be a great addition to your paper and provide strong support for your claim. But it's easy to get carried away, so that everything – even the most mundane sentence from an article – is a direct quote. When this happens, the results are: (1) no quote becomes important, because everything is quoted, and nothing "stands out" to the reader; (2) the quotations aren't effectively integrated into the paper, making them less likely to support the claim; and (3) the author, just by inserting a quotation here and there, may not fully understand the testimony or what it means in the context of his or her argument.

Instead, paraphrasing is usually the better way to work testimony into a paper. I understand the word "testimony" conjures something you might not feel comfortable paraphrasing. "Testimony," for example, may make some people think of witnesses at a trial, or someone's story told in a church setting. Obviously, those things shouldn't be paraphrased; the exact words used by the person "testifying" are meant to be heard as is. Rarely, however, does expert testimony from an author in a research article, or a story from a magazine or newspaper, fall into this category. In general, your first inclination should be to paraphrase sentences or passages taken from articles, newspapers, magazines, and any other source you might cite as support your claim. Table 3.3 provides some general guidelines to help you know when to paraphrase and when to quote directly.

Using quotations in a sentence   So, let's say you look over Table 3.3 and decide the sentence or passage you want to use in your paper merits quoting directly. How do you quote it? If you read enough published articles and enough of your classmates' papers, you'll find many possible ways to directly quote something,

Table 3.3 How to incorporate testimony in a paper

Type of testimony	How to incorporate into paper
Sentence expresses a basic point in mundane language (e.g., "The number of homes devastated by natural disasters has increased by 3% over the last ten years.")	**Paraphrase**: While the evidence itself may be necessary to support your argument, there is nothing unique about the language that requires quoting the author directly.
Sentence expresses the author's personal experience in a situation (e.g., "When I surveyed the damage to my home, I wondered how I would rebuild.")	It depends… **Paraphrase**: If the author's experience is important to your claim, but the language used isn't poetic and doesn't have strong imagery, then you should paraphrase. **Quote directly**: If the author's words are poetic or use imagery vital to the experience, then you should quote directly.
Sentence uses imagery and other unique language to express the author's opinion or experience (e.g., "As I looked around at the home we built torn in two, I felt like I had been punched in the gut and had the wind knocked out of me.")	**Quote directly**: The author's use of language is vital to understanding the testimony, therefore you should quote directly.

some effective and some not so effective. First, let's go over the not-so-effective ways to quote directly.

As you probably know, regardless of the citation style you're required to use, you need to put quotation marks around anything you want to quote directly:

- "This is the sentence or phrase you want to quote directly."

While we may often think that the period goes inside the quotation marks, it's usually *not* the case, as you'll be putting the citation (author, year, page number) in parentheses after the quotation and *then* using a period. We'll go over citation styles later in this chapter, so for now let's focus on *integrating* the quotation into a paragraph. The problem a lot of writers encounter is what to put before and after the quotation. The most *ineffective* way is to just drop it in between two sentences, like this:

- These are your original words. "This is the sentence or phrase you want to quote directly." These are more of your original words.

What's wrong with this? Well, sometimes the reader may not understand how what you're quoting fits into your argument. Consider this example from a student's paper about communication in the bicycling community. While I'm quoting this student's paper directly, I have only included the quotation marks around the direct quotation from this student's source:

> Most communities have realized the importance of bicycle commuting as a viable transportation alternative. "Americans have grown more and more accustomed to their automobiles. That's why Bike to Work Day

(3rd day in May) was created and then expanded to Bike to Work Week (3rd week in May)"

(NCDOT, n.d., para. 6).

Notice that the quotation itself, just dropped in after the first sentence in the author's own words, doesn't seem to fully support the author's argument. If most communities have realized the important of bicycling, then why, as the source says, should it be the case that more and more Americans use automobiles? Granted, it makes sense that bicycle advocates would want to create a Bike to Work Week, but the quotation as it's presented in the student's paper seems to contradict the author's argument. And without the student's own words explaining how this quotation supports his arguments, readers may be confused.

So, how does the author fix this? Well, for starters, this quotation doesn't seem to fit the criteria we established for directly quoting a source: the language itself is fairly mundane and should be paraphrased. But, let's assume for the moment that the source did warrant a direct quotation. How could this quotation be more effectively integrated into the passage so that it supports the author's argument? The first rule of thumb is to *always lead into or follow up a direct quotation in your own words – in the same sentence.* This means inserting a phrase like "The authors argue…" or "As Smith argues…" A follow-up in your own words means putting something in at the end of the sentence, like "[quotation], argues Smith."

Let's go back to the author's original passage and rewrite it adhering to this guideline, with the added revisions tinted gray:

> Most communities have realized the importance of bicycle commuting as a viable transportation alternative. Despite this, the automobile is still the primary mode of transportation. The North Carolina Department of Transportation website explains how bicycle advocates reacted, noting that "Americans have grown more and more accustomed to their automobiles. That's why Bike to Work Day (3rd day in May) was created and then expanded to Bike to Work Week (3rd week in May)." *(NCDOT, 2014, para. 6).*

Alternatively, the author could have followed the quotation with his own tag line that also contextualized the quotation in relation to the argument being presented. This revised tag line (with a one word addition at the beginning of the passage) is tinted gray:

> Although most communities have realized the importance of bicycle commuting as a viable transportation alternative, "Americans have grown more and more accustomed to their automobiles. That's why Bike to Work Day (3rd day in May) was created and then expanded to Bike to Work Week (3rd week in May)," explains The North Carolina Department of Transportation website. *(NCDOT, 2014, para. 6).*

While not as smooth as the first instance, in both cases the quotation is easier to understand in relation to the author's argument because the student included a lead-in or follow-up to the direct quotation *in his own words.*

In short, when using direct quotations in a sentence, always lead in to or follow up the quotation (in the same sentence) with your own words. Doing this allows you to contextualize the quotation, frame it in relation to your argument, and make sure there is no confusion as to how it supports your argument. Of course, you can avoid all of this by paraphrasing the testimony in the first place. In the above example, it's clear that the passage doesn't need to be directly quoted; there is nothing poetic about the sentence, and it doesn't contain vivid imagery or figures of speech. When this is the case, as it will usually be with most passages cited in a class paper, you should choose to paraphrase *instead* of quote directly.

Using paraphrasing in a sentence   A note of instruction I give to all my students is for a paper that is roughly 10–12 pages in length. They should have *no more than 3 direct quotations* unless they are citing from an interview they conducted, field notes they took, or from an artifact they are analyzing (such as a speech or film). Understandably, students are initially shocked at this stringent guideline. However, their papers ultimately read much better because they are forced to comprehend the source they are citing and integrate it into their argument in a more cohesive way by paraphrasing the evidence.

Let's take the student example from above and imagine the passage were paraphrased rather than quoted directly, with the paraphrased portion tinted gray:

> Most communities have realized the importance of bicycle commuting as a viable transportation alternative. Overall, however, a majority of Americans are still heavily dependent on their automobiles. To raise awareness, the League of American Bicyclists created Bike to Work Day, which soon became Bike to Work Week. *(NCDOT, 2014, para. 6).*

There are a few improvements in the paraphrasing in this passage. First, the passage better supports the author's argument; we understand *why* bike awareness is still necessary even though, according to the student author, most communities have realized the importance of bicycle commuting. Second, the passage reads more smoothly, and the source citation is less obtrusive. Notice that even with paraphrasing, the source is still cited.

We can apply this guideline for paraphrasing to any type of evidence we cite for our argument: statistics, examples, illustrations, or testimony. Our major concern for citing evidence should be that we provide backing for our overall claim, and that the reader understands how this evidence fits into the overall picture of our argument (Figure 3.1).

If we take a final look at the student example, we may begin to wonder some things about the argument itself. For example, are these Bike Awareness Weeks meant to convert drivers into bicycle riders? If communities have recognized the importance of bicycling, what does this mean? Bike lanes? Are there other equally "green" methods of transportation? What about carpooling? Won't that cut down on traffic and pollution? All these questions are related to the *warrant* (Toulmin 2003) in the Toulmin Model of creating and analyzing arguments.

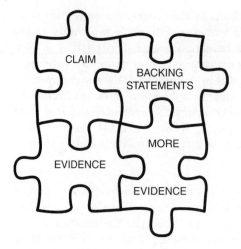

Figure 3.1 Puzzle with pieces labeled

Warrants: Often unstated, always important

In the Toulmin Model, the *warrant* is the often unstated, but sometimes explicit, chain of reasoning that connects the claim, the backing or support statements, and the evidence. As I explained at the beginning of the chapter, arguments are something we make in our everyday lives, for example, movie or television show recommendations. So, just to be consistent, let's revisit our movie recommendation to a friend in some imagined dialogue, each element of which is labeled with a part of the Toulmin Model:

YOU: You should see this movie. [*Claim*]
FRIEND: Why?
YOU: Because it's really good. [*Reason or Backing*]
FRIEND: Why is it "really good"?
YOU: It's got a lot of action, it's fast-paced, and it's pretty funny. [*Evidence*]*

This last statement with an asterisk (*) isn't actually spoken, but it's implied. In this imagined dialogue, the implication is that, by using the examples of "action" and "humor" as evidence to support your claim, you believe these two criteria are necessary in a good movie. This chain of reasoning is called the *warrant*. Recognizing warrants is vital when analyzing the arguments of others, but especially when creating our own arguments.

It's helpful to be aware of the warrant when creating our arguments because we don't want to imply something we don't believe is true or accurate. In the above example, let's say you don't really believe that action and humor are two criteria of a good movie. If so, you will probably want to find other evidence to support the claim that this movie is a good movie. There are

---

*What qualifies a movie to be "good," according to you, is that it is full of action and humor. [*Warrant*]

many different types of warrants, and we'll cover just a few of them below to help you get a better sense of warrants. With each type of warrant covered, I also discuss some related *logical fallacies* to help you ensure that your reasoning is sound.

Generalization and sign

"Generalization," a common term in social science research and quantitative reasoning, refers to the ability to apply findings or conclusions about a smaller sample or set of items to the larger population or broader set of the same type of items. When you use a warrant of *generalization*, you imply or (sometimes) explicitly state that your claim and evidentiary reasoning are sound because what you claim is true can be generalized to a broader set of items or population.

Let's go back to the imagined dialogue above. Let's say you haven't seen the movie in question but would like to go see it because it stars the great American actress Meryl Streep. You might tell your friend, "We should go see this movie [*Claim*] because Meryl Streep is in it [*Reason or Backing*]." The *Warrant* in this argument – that films with Meryl Streep in them are usually worth seeing – is one of generalization. In other words, you are making a generalization about all Meryl Streep films based on the ones you yourself have seen. So, although you haven't seen the newest film starring her, you assume it will be good – and make an argument based on this warrant – because you've seen her other films and believe them to be good.

Reasoning by *sign* is also included in this section because it's similar to reasoning by generalization. When we reason using a sign, we are following the thought pattern, "Where's there's smoke, there's fire." In this common phrase, smoke is assumed to be *sign* of fire. Going back to our movie recommendation example, we could conclude based on the warrant in that argument that Meryl Streep's presence is the *sign* of a good movie.

Logical fallacy: Hasty generalization

With reasoning from generalization or sign, there are some *logical fallacies* you should be sure to avoid. A common fallacy with reasoning from generalization and sign is *hasty generalization*. To understand if you're committing this fallacy, you must ask yourself, "Am I generalizing based on one piece of evidence?" In our hypothetical movie example, the person recommending the movie might ask themselves, "If Meryl Streep has been in many good films, is it accurate to generalize to all her films?" With this particular actor, we have more than enough evidence, but that may not be the case for other subjects covered in the papers we write for our classes.

Authority

The next type of warrant reasoning has to do with appeals to expert opinion. Arguing from *authority* is pretty much what it sounds like: basing our reasoning on the presence of an authority figure or a statement of evidence from an expert or someone in authority. If we were to slightly change our argument about recommending a film, it's clear that arguing from authority – or using authority as the reasoning in our warrant – is a common type of argument we make every day. This example below includes that reasoning in gray tint:

YOU: You should see this movie. [*Claim*]

FRIEND: Why?

YOU: Because it's gotten good reviews. [*Reason or Backing*]

FRIEND: What did these reviews say?

YOU: Well, the local movie critic said it was fast-paced and funny and gave it a good review. [*Evidence*]*

In this argument, the reason or backing for a movie being "good" is that it's gotten positive reviews. The evidence used is a review written by the local movie critic. This critic's expertise is the *authority* in this warrant. By using the movie critic's review as evidence, you are implying that the critic knows what she's talking about and can be trusted. Of course, other types of "authority" could be used. For example, you might cite the "fresh" percentage from the Rotten Tomatoes reviews website. Implicit in this argument – the reasoning behind the warrant – is that the majority of the general movie-going public can be trusted to make sound judgments on what is and is not a good film.

Logical fallacy: Appeal to authority

Just as with our previous type of warrant, we have to be careful not to commit a logical fallacy. The danger in reasoning from authority is, rather confusingly, called an *appeal to authority*. Simply, this logical fallacy occurs when we uncritically appeal to authority: just because someone tells us to do something doesn't mean we should do it. If that person is a legitimate authority on something, or a credible figure or expert in the area, then fine, no problem. However, if we're arguing that others should do or think something just because some random person in authority says so (regardless of that person's knowledge or expertise), that's the logical fallacy of *appeal to authority*.

Principle

The last type of reasoning for the warrant we'll cover is *reasoning from principle*. Think of this type of reasoning as based on a widely accepted assumption. For example, in our imagined dialogue above, we might question whether going to see movies in a movie theater is even desirable anymore. It costs a lot, and we can now access a lot of movies on demand in the comfort of our own home, and watch movies on Netflix or a similar type of service. The *principle* here is an assumption that this film should be experienced in a movie theatre. Let's combine the backing and the evidence and take another look at our dialogue, with changes in red:

YOU: You should see this movie while it's in theaters. [*Claim with qualifier*]

FRIEND: Why?

YOU: Because it's got great special effects, like robots fighting over the city in mid-air. [*Reason or Backing, and Evidence*]**

---

* What qualifies a movie as "good" is that an authority figure – the film critic – gave it a positive review. [*Warrant*]

** Certain types of movies are just better when seen on the big screen. [*Warrant*]

The principle or common assumption behind this warrant is that certain elements of a film, like the special effects, are best viewed on the big screen of a movie theater as opposed to one's television screen (regardless of how big that is). Your friend may not agree with your warrant, and therefore reject your claim and argument (or make a *counterclaim*, such as "I can enjoy movies at home and I'm not spending the money").

Logical fallacy: Begging the question

There's no one logical fallacy that readily accompanies this type of warrant. However, a common fallacy that might occur with reasoning from principle is *begging the question*. In this fallacy, the common assumption in the warrant is taken to be a truth or fact. In our movie recommendation, the assumption is that special effects make a film great. Of course, many people may disagree with this, yet the recommender may believe this assumption is true for everyone. Notice that this is just assumed in the argument with no question; hence, it's "begging" to be questioned.

   Another everyday occurrence of this fallacy might take place in your very own classroom. For example, you might question your instructor about a grade you received in class:

YOU:	I don't understand why I received a B on this assignment.
INSTRUCTOR:	Because, according to the grading rubric, it didn't quite meet the standards of A work in this class.

Now, the reasoning from principle warrant in this dialogue is the common assumption that grading rubrics provide a rigorous marker of whether an assignment meets certain learning outcomes for the class. But the instructor – who certainly isn't perfect or all-knowing – writes the rubrics. Since the instructor wrote the rubric on which your assignment was graded, he's essentially saying "I gave you a B because it was a B paper." That's sounds like nonsense, right? Hopefully, an instructor would give you a more thoughtful response. And I'm not advocating that you argue with your teacher about a grade. But this is an example of *begging the question*. The notion that the rubric is a good indicator of paper quality is unquestioned; but when we break down the argument, we can see this assumption is begging to be questioned. This is a common fallacy and a difficult one to catch, simply because its circular reasoning is often embedded in the claim itself.

Student Spotlight: Making Claims

To better understand making arguments in a paper, let's take a look at an argument an actual student of mine made in her paper. This is a data-driven undergraduate research paper that draws on interviews and observations of a Deaf community that gathers weekly to network and socialize. This student, Jessica, makes the following claim in her introduction: "The consequential numbers of people affected by hearing loss in our country calls for more research into the phenomenon of audism and its effects on communication within the Deaf community." If you recall our discussion of types of claims earlier in this chapter, you may be thinking, "This sounds like a claim of policy because it suggests a course of action or change of some kind." If so, then you'd be correct. In this case, the course of action is actually a call for more research on *audism*, or the idea that being able to hear makes a person superior to someone who cannot hear (Harrington and Jacobi 2009). This claim also contains a backing statement, but for now, let's consider it as a whole.

While Jessica could have made a stronger claim based on the data she gathered in her paper, for example: *Communication in Deaf community groups like the one studied creates unique norms that foster cohesion among members and resist the norms put upon them by the mainstream hearing community*, her claim is still a sound one. So, let's examine the warrant in this claim by putting it into the dialogue format we used with the hypothetical film recommendation. Let's pretend you are having a conversation with Jessica:

JESSICA: There needs to be more research on audism and the Deaf community. [*Claim*]
YOU: Why?
JESSICA: There are growing numbers of people affected by hearing loss. [A *Backing Statement* for which we assume she'll provide evidence]*

The implied warrant is something with which most people, at least your teachers, would agree. We might conclude that this warrant contains reasoning from principle because she's assuming that research by experts on a topic is a good thing. Is this the point of Jessica's paper, though? It's certainly one of the main take-aways, but my rewritten claim above – *Communication in Deaf community groups like the one studied creates unique norms that foster cohesion among members and resist the norms put upon them by the mainstream hearing community* – is more in line with what the data in her paper ultimately supports. Nonetheless, there are no logical fallacies in her warrant, as it's probably safe to assume that the value of research by experts on a topic is widely accepted among readers.

Whether your claim is about data you yourself have gathered, or about the state of research on a particular phenomenon, writing sound claims with backing statements connected by a well-thought-out warrant provides a solid foundation for your paper. Hopefully, remembering that arguments are something you use in your everyday life will help when formulating your arguments for whatever paper you have to write for class.

Now that you're an expert in making claims and understand the relationship between claims, evidence, and warrants, you may be wondering how to put this all together. We'll talk more about style and formatting in Chapter 4. For now, we're going to cover an essential part of using evidence to support any argument: citing sources.

---

* Scholarly research like this paper can help with this issue in some way. [*Warrant*]

Write Away

Take your argument for the paper you're writing and break it down into dialogue like the examples in this chapter:

> *Claim*:
> [Ask why]
> *Reason or Backing Statement*:
> [Ask why or so what]
> *Evidence*:

As you do this, be sure to pay attention to the warrant, or the implied assumption that links your reasons and evidence with your claim. Then consider: Does this imagined dialogue make sense? Would you believe it?

Common Citation Styles

You can have a sound claim, and great backing for your claim, but no reader will trust what you're saying if it doesn't seem like you're *credible*. And one of the most important parts of credibility on paper (as opposed to speaking in front of audiences, when you can rely on your nonverbal skills to enhance your credibility) is **properly citing your sources**. The primary reason for citing your sources is to enable your readers to look up the sources you use so they can better evaluate your argument. Of course, no reader is likely to do this unless: (1) it's your instructor, and she wants to find the context for a direct quotation or citation; or (2) another student is reading your paper and wants to cite the same source as you. Regardless, properly citing your sources in the correct format can go a long way toward increasing your credibility as a writer, not to mention that proper source citations are usually an important part of the grade for any paper you write.

Below, we're going to cover three of the most common citation styles used in the social sciences and humanities. It's important to remember that you often won't be able to choose the citation style; your instructor or, should you get your paper published, editor will prefer a particular style. For example, I usually write in APA or MLA style but had to learn Chicago style in writing this book. I've taught a lot of students who are frustrated at having to learn more than one citation style during their college careers, but I think by understanding some of the reasoning behind each, the basics of each style will be easier to grasp. It's also crucial to keep in mind that each of these styles has its own separate manual you can purchase. We're only going to cover the basics below, but you may have some more in-depth questions that can only be answered by going directly to each manual (see Further Reading).

APA

The American Psychological Association (APA) published its first set of guidelines for authors in a 1929 newsletter. Pressured by the increasing professionalization of the discipline, meaning that there was a growing number of psychology practitioners both inside and outside of the academy, the APA put forth guidelines to standardize the reporting of scientific studies so editors, reviewers, authors, and readers would all be on the "same page" when it came to discussing and building on each other's research. Today, we have a set of guidelines that do much the same thing, encompassing online sources in addition to common and uncommon print sources. For the purposes of your class papers, you'll most likely need to know a few basics.

So, let's begin at the end, with the References page that will usually appear at the end of your research paper. APA guidelines specify that this must be labeled "References" at the top of the first page of your list of sources (as opposed to other styles, such as MLA's, which recommends "Works Cited"). A standard References page entry will usually be an academic journal article or a book. Let's examine a journal article citation, annotated with the most important APA terms. In order to better understand the order of each item, we'll go over them one by one (see Figure 3.2).

Name

It's important to note that *only the first initial of the first name* appears in this reference. Since this is one of my articles, I'll use myself as an example. You know my first name – it's on the cover of this book. Why isn't it included here? Remember the desire for standardization that prompted APA guidelines in the first place? Well, that standardization also communicates certain values about the approach of social science research: it shouldn't matter who conducted the study, and their ethnicity, gender, etc. should not play a role in the evaluation of their research. As such, the first name of the researcher isn't important in terms of the research; good science is good science, we shouldn't care if the author is male or female, and we shouldn't have to guess at the ethnicity because neither has any bearing on the quality of research.

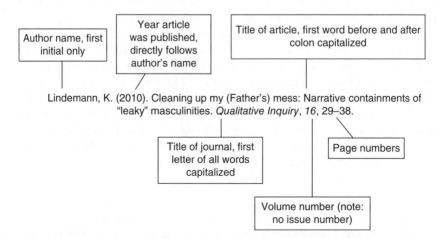

Figure 3.2 APA reference annotation

Year

Next in order is the year. Why does the year come second when other styles place the year near the end of the citation? Because when evaluating good social scientific research, we need to know the author is up to date on the latest research. Citations about trends in social media, for example, will be more credible if they are from the last year as opposed to five years ago. Think about how quickly social media platforms come and go. A year before writing this book, I would not have known about Yik Yak. Now, there are many articles about its uses and misuses among U.S. college students (see Mahler 2015, for example). Granted, other concepts and topics may not be as time-sensitive (relational conflict unfortunately seems to be a timeless topic, for example). But in general, because the year of the research is important, APA specifies that it come right after the name, both on the References page and in the in-text citation (more on that below).

Title of article or chapter

After the name with the first initial and the year, the title of the article itself appears. Note that only the first letter in the title (and after the colon) is capitalized. Believe it or not, this is meant to make things easier on you as you type the reference. Only having to capitalize the first letter should make things go quicker when typing the title, right? That's what the people at APA think.

Journals and books

Perhaps counterintuitively, then, every word of the journal is capitalized. But remember, in the social sciences, which value peer-reviewed journal articles (arguably even more than books), the journal title is one of the most important item in the reference. As such, its importance is displayed prominently by capitalizing every word of the journal's name. Conversely, the title of a book is treated the same way the title of a journal article is capitalizing only the first word of the title and the first word after any colons.

Volume, issue, page numbers

The *volume* is basically the yearly output of a journal. For example, if a journal was founded in 2013, then Volume 1 would be all the journal *issues* published in 2013; there might be four issues in Volume 1, with each issue published in three-month increments (January, April, July, and November). Volume 2 would then refer to all issues published in 2014, and so on. If we could communicate face to face right now, I would bet you that when creating an APA-correct reference for a References page, you will almost *never* enter the issue number of a journal's volume. And 95% of the time, I'd win the bet. If you take another look at the annotated reference above, you'll see there's no issue number. You'll find this is true with almost any APA reference.

Why aren't issues numbers included? One simple reason: *continuous pagination*. Okay, maybe it's not that simple, but allow me to explain. Usually every page of the *volume* of a journal is numbered *consecutively*. This means that the first issue of every *volume* starts with page 1 and continues until the last page of the last issue of that same volume. There's only one page 23 in each entire volume of a journal (which could be four issues, each issue with 100 pages). Because this is the case, you don't need the issue number in which an article appeared. The page number is sufficient to help a reader find the original source you're citing in your paper. A more recent trend has been to simply include the issue number so readers can better find it online, so adherence to this rule may not be as strictly enforced as other APA rules. Check with your instructor for clarification on including issue numbers.

In-text citations

Of course, you can't include references on a References page and not cite them in your paper (and vice versa). There are a few hard and fast rules here as well. First and foremost, *the year always follows the author's name*. This is true whether the author's name appears in the sentence proper – "Lindemann (2010) explains…" – or if it only appears in parentheses, for example: "Disability and masculinity have several important intersections (Lindemann, 2010)." Notice that, in each case, the year always follows the author name. If you include a direct quotation from the article or book, *you must always include the page number* with a "p." in front: (p. 10).

MLA

APA style is perhaps the most common citation style used in communication classes and other social science courses like psychology, anthropology, and sociology. Arguably, the second most used style, especially in communication classes that feature rhetoric or performance studies, as well as history and English classes, is MLA (Modern Language Association) style. The "MLA Style Sheet" was first published in 1951. The differences between APA and MLA are important, and can be easily understood by simply thinking about the *types* of research commonly cited in each style.

As I briefly explained above, APA is most often used in the social sciences. MLA is usually used in the humanities disciplines, such as history, English, and communication (in certain areas such as rhetoric and performance studies). Usually, the disciplines associated with the humanities draw on and analyze texts, documents, and speeches that are important regardless of how recently they were published. Important novels by Ernest Hemingway or Edith Wharton, a speech by Abraham Lincoln, a Shakespeare play, and even government documents may be cited by scholars writing in the humanities. When you consider this, things like an author's *name* become much more important, while things like the *year* of publication may be less important.

As with APA style, we're going to address each MLA item one by one. But Figure 3.3 shows what the previous citation would look like in MLA style on a Works Cited (instead of a References) page:

Name

It matters who gave a speech or wrote a novel. Sometimes, the race and gender of the speaker or author can help us better analyze that text and its meaning. We wouldn't shorten Susan B. Anthony's name to "Anthony, S. B." when citing one of her speeches advocating for U.S. women's right to vote. To better

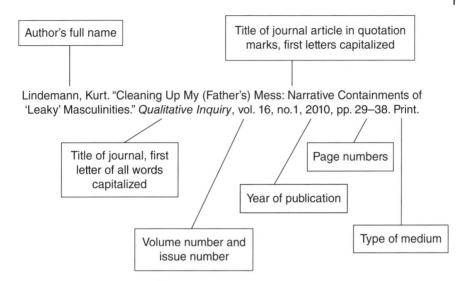

Figure 3.3 MLA reference annotation

understand that speech, readers need to know that it was a woman who had the courage to get arrested for trying to vote and then speaking to the public about it in 1872. Likewise, literary works are often analyzed based on the gender and race of the author. For example, David Unaipon (David Ngunaitponi) was the first indigenous Australian to be published in that country in the early 20th century. His heritage is important in assessing his contributions to Australian culture, and we would want to be sure his entire name is featured in the Works Cited page.

Year

Although the name of an author is important, the year may not always be. Remember that for APA style and social science research, it's important that readers know the research cited is up to date; that's part of the foundation of social science – using the best available research and data. For MLA, the reasoning is a little different. For example, unless someone is a Shakespeare scholar comparing editions of his works, the year the play *Hamlet* was published may not be of utmost importance to us and our readers. As such, you can see the year of a published work comes much later in the MLA Works Cited reference.

Titles of articles, journals, and books

The title of the article appears near the beginning of the reference, just as in APA. However, in MLA every first letter is capitalized and the title has quotation marks around it. If you think of a short story or poem you've read (or were *forced* to read) for a class, you may recall that these often appear with quotation marks around them. In a nod to the importance of such literary works, MLA style also has the title capitalized and in quotation marks. The capitalization and italicization of the title of the journal or book is the same as with APA.

Volume, issue, page numbers

Another major difference between APA and MLA lies in the representation of issue numbers. We've already discussed why issue numbers don't usually appear in APA references. As you can see in the above example, in MLA style they do. Why is this? Well, earlier editions of MLA required this, as does APA, when continuously paginated journal issues were not cited. This has changed with the most recent eighth edition as of the writing of this chapter. The reasoning for this change is to make it easier for you, the writer: now, you don't have to figure out whether a journal is continuously paginated to know whether to include the issue number on the Works Cited – you just include the issue number regardless.

In-text citations

The in-text citations for MLA style are similar to those in APA style with a few exceptions. First, the year of the publication doesn't appear in the text. Additionally, no "p" appears in the parentheses before the page number. So, an in-text citation from the article I've used as an example might read: "Disability and masculinity have several important intersections (Lindemann 30)." Importantly, while APA doesn't require a page number if you paraphrase, only when providing a direct quotation, MLA dictates that you *must always* provide a page number when quoting *or* paraphrasing.

Chicago

The Chicago style of documentation, sometimes called Turabian style (when geared particularly toward student research papers, theses, and dissertations), is used in both the humanities and social sciences, and is the preferred documentation style for "real world" book writers (which includes yours truly writing this textbook!). Why would you use this style instead of APA or MLA? Ultimately, it depends on your instructor, but some have described Chicago style as less intrusive for the reader than MLA or APA styles. Chicago is the oldest of the three styles here, dating all the way back to 1891 when the University of Chicago Press first began publishing books (University of Chicago Press Staff 2010).

Chicago style has also been called the most comprehensive of the three styles covered here. In fact, there are two forms of documentation associated with Chicago style: the Notes-Bibliographic (NB) system, used primarily in the areas of literature, art, and history, and the Author-Date or Parenthetical References system, used in the social sciences. Since the latter is likely what you'll use if asked to use Chicago style, we're going to focus on the Author-Date or Parenthetical References system. Let's begin (again) with the article we've been using as an example, noting the differences between this style of the previous two (see Figure 3.4).

Note that the style in Figure 3.4 looks very similar to MLA style. At the end of your paper (when using the Author-Date system), these kinds of references would appear on a "References" page (not a "Works Cited" page as with MLA). If you're using the NB system, this source citation would appear in a footnote and in a "Bibliography" page at the end of your paper. On this Bibliography page, it

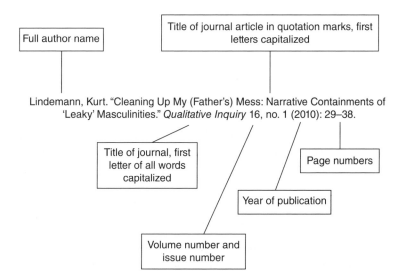

Figure 3.4 Chicago reference annotation

would look exactly the same as above. However, when providing a footnote, it would appear differently. Let's discuss those differences below.

In-text citations

The major difference between Chicago and the other two styles we've covered so far is the way the sources are cited in the text of the paper. Let's go over the Author-Date system first, as it's similar to APA style. If you were citing the journal article in Figure 3.4 in your paper, it would simply read: (Lindemann, 2010). When paraphrasing or quoting directly from a source, the page number appears with *no* "p" (similar to MLA): Kurt Lindemann argues that "[quotation]" (31).

In the NB system, you simply include a footnote at the end of the quotation or paraphrase, and then put the source at the bottom of the page (the end of the document but before the Bibliography if you're using endnotes instead of footnotes – ask your instructor if you're unsure as to which is the preferred notes method). The first time you cite the source in a footnote, it should be cued with a superior figure like this,[1] and the note should appear at the bottom of the page:

1. Kurt Lindemann, "Cleaning Up My (Father's) Mess: Narrative Containments of 'Leaky' Masculinities." *Qualitative Inquiry* 16, no. 1 (2010): [the page number to which you're referring].

If you cite it again immediately after,[2] then it would look like this:

2. Ibid., [page number, if you're referring to a particular passage].

The term "Ibid." is short for the Latin word *ibidem*, which means "in the same place." It makes sense to use this abbreviation as you are directing readers to the same article you just cited, and it's shorter than constantly writing "See the same article" in your footnotes.

Now, if you cite an article on one page and then cite it again on another page, you don't have to type the complete source again. Instead, it should look like this[3] at the bottom of the page:

3. Lindemann, "'Leaky' Masculinities," 31.

Note the shortened article title (choose a few unique identifying terms) and the just the last name.

Understanding the various source citation styles discussed in this chapter is a good start in the fight against plagiarism. However, simply knowing how to cite sources isn't enough. In the box "Engaging Ethics," I offer a more detailed discussion of an ethical approach to citing sources.

Engaging Ethics

Plagiarism is a common concern among college instructors. Your school no doubt has a policy on plagiarism, and you may even have such a policy listed in your course syllabus. While some instructors use plagiarism prevention software, like Turnitin.com, others may simply Google suspicious-looking passages. In fact, a simple Google search will reveal that several university administrators have been accused of plagiarism recently!

What are some causes of plagiarism? Stress and perceived lack of time. Believe it or not, one of the most common reasons my students have given me when I note something in their paper that's suspiciously similar to another passage is that they were stressed from other assignments and just wanted a shortcut to finishing their paper.

So, how do you avoid plagiarism? Here are a few simple steps you can take:

- Paraphrase whenever possible. Follow the guidelines earlier in this chapter. If the language is unique (metaphor, figure of speech, imagery, etc.) then quote. Otherwise, paraphrase.
- Ask your instructor if you can submit drafts to Turnitin.com or another type of software before submitting your final version. If you can, submit a draft early and look at the report. Sometimes we don't mean to copy another source verbatim; we may be so familiar with our sources that it just happens. And when it does – and when we catch it before the final draft – we can easily change the language.
- Google a random passage of your paper and see what comes up. If you notice more than four unique words in a row (*not* "the," "of," or "and") then change your own language.

Chapter Summary

In this chapter we've talked about how to identify arguments in any paper by first recognizing the ways we use arguments in our everyday conversations. Then, using the Toulmin Method, we discussed the types of claims you might make in an argument, as well as how to provide backing for your arguments. Remember that backing for arguments includes the warrant – the often unspoken and unwritten reasoning that connects the claim and the evidence. We also briefly covered the most common types of research citation styles you might encounter in your classes: APA, MLA, and Chicago styles. Remember to seek out the manuals for each style for more detailed information. There are also great online resources for citations, one of the best and most popular being the "Purdue Owl." Finally, I've identified some common citation mistakes that lead to plagiarism and some ways to prevent it.

Remember that you already know how to make an argument; you likely do it on an almost daily basis. Now, the next time you make a movie or television show recommendation to friends, can you provide sound backing and evidence to convince them to watch it?

References

Bitzer, Lloyd F. 1968. "The Rhetorical Situation." *Philosophy and Rhetoric*, 1 (1): 1–14.

Cialdini, Robert B. 2007. *Influence: The Psychology of Persuasion*. New York: HarperCollins.

Curtis, Richard, dir. 2003. *Love, Actually*. Film. Universal City, CA: Universal. DVD, 2004.

Foss, Sonja K., and Griffin, Cindy. 1995. "Beyond Persuasion: A Proposal for Invitational Rhetoric." *Communication Monographs*, 62: 2–18.

Fowler, E. Ramsey, and Aaron, Jane E. (2011). *The Little, Brown Handbook* (12th ed.). London: Longman.

Goleman, Daniel. 2013. *Focus: The Hidden Driver of Excellence*. New York: Harper.

Griffin, Cindy. 2011. *Invitation to Public Speaking*. Boston, MA: Wadsworth.

Harrington, Tom, and Jacobi, Cindy. 2009. "What is Audism: Introduction." Last modified April 2009. Accessed November 10, 2016 from http://libguides. gallaudet.edu/content.php?pid=114455&sid=989379.

Kennedy, George A. 1991. *Aristotle, On Rhetoric. A Theory of Civic Discourse*. Oxford: Oxford University Press.

Mahler, Jonathan. 2015. "Who Spewed That Abuse? Anonymous Yik Yak App Isn't Telling," *The New York Times*, March 8. Accessed June 2, 2015 from http://www. nytimes.com/2015/03/09/technology/popular-yik-yak-app-confers-anonymity- and-delivers-abuse.html?_r=0.

North Carolina Department of Transportation. 2014. "Types of Cycling." Accessed November 28 2015 from http://www.ncdot.gov/bikeped/bicycle/types/.

Purdue Owl. 2014. "Organizing Your Argument." Last modified November 6, 2014. Accessed November 10, 2016 from https://owl.english.purdue.edu/owl/ resource/588/03/.

Stiff, James B., and Mongeau, Paul. 2003. *Persuasive Communication*. New York: Guilford Press.

Toulmin, Stephen E. 2003. *The Uses of Argument* (updated ed.). Cambridge, UK: Cambridge University Press.

University of Chicago Press Staff. 2010. "The History of the Chicago Manual of Style." Accessed June 3, 2015 from http://www.chicagomanualofstyle.org/ about16_history.html.

Watson, Leon. 2015. "Humans Have Shorter Attention Span Than Goldfish, Thanks to Smartphones," *The Telegraph*, May 13. Accessed June 1, 2015 from http://www.telegraph.co.uk/news/science/science-news/11607315/Humans-have-shorter-attention-span-than-goldfish-thanks-to-smartphones.html.

Further Reading

APA (American Psychological Association). 2009. *Publication Manual of the American Psychological Association* (6th ed.). Washington, DC: APA.

MLA (Modern Language Association). 2009. *MLA Handbook for Writers of Research Papers* (7th ed.). New York: MLA.

The Stanford Encyclopedia online has some easy-to-read material on Aristotle and rhetoric: http://plato.stanford.edu/entries/aristotle-rhetoric/#agenda.

University of Chicago Press Staff. 2010. *The Chicago Manual of Style* (17th ed). Chicago, IL: University of Chicago Press.

4

Style and Format: How to Say What You Want to Say

Chapter Learning Outcomes

- Distinguish between effective uses of voice
- Identify the parts of a well-written paragraph
- Employ effective topic sentences
- Write coherent and cohesive paragraphs
- Visualize effective paragraphs as part of an overall argument

Composing Research, Communicating Results: Writing the Communication Research Paper,
First Edition. Kurt Lindemann.
© 2018 John Wiley & Sons, Inc. Published 2018 by John Wiley & Sons, Inc.

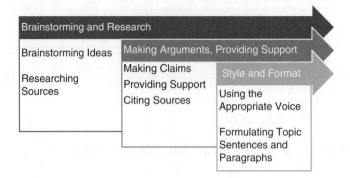

Figure 4.1 The paper-writing process

Chapter Features

- Student Spotlight
- "Write Away"

In Chapter 1, we discussed the spark of understanding between a reader and author when the author effectively communicates her ideas. We begin this chapter with the metaphor of a spark, and take it a bit further. If the brainstorming is the spark of the paper, we might consider the writing style the transistors and wires that carry the current of ideas that runs through your paper. For example, each paragraph carries that current to the next paragraph until, at the end of the section or paper, you've illuminated some idea or argument for your readers. Each paragraph contains stylistic choices that can alter the current, redirect it, and even short-circuit it (Figure 4.1).

The Purpose of This Chapter

In this chapter, we'll focus on the various components that contribute to the overall style of an academic paper. We'll discuss voice, thesis sentences, the elusive "flow" of a paper, topic sentences and paragraph structure, and figures of speech and grammar. As we consider the various parts of an overall style, I'd like you to reflect on your own writing and the degree to which you put care, effort, and thoughtfulness into each sentence of your paper.

Your Voice, Your Audience

Just like a speech or presentation, an academic paper demands careful consideration of the audience; this is key to crafting your voice. And just like in a public speaking class, your audience for your class paper is composed of other students, who might have some knowledge about your topic, and your instructor, who likely has more knowledge about the topic, theory, and concepts you're discussing. So, what does this mean for your tone of voice? Should it be formal or informal?

Can you use first person ("I")? Should you refer to yourself as "the researcher" like some of the scholarly articles you've read for class? Of course, the answer to these questions depends in part on your instructor and the class. So, you should first ask your instructor and consult the syllabus and any grading rubrics. Regardless, at some point in your academic writing career you'll be expected to make your own choices about voice. This section will help you consider the ramifications of choosing a particular voice.

As you read this section, remember that these are *options*, and that *you* must decide which options are best suited to the three demands we covered in Chapter 1: Topic, Audience, and Occasion. The topic of your paper may influence your choice of voice in whatever *type* of writing you're doing: Is it a personal e-mail to employees? Are you expected to write about yourself or your reactions to a particular reading, film, or theory for a class paper? The audience you're writing for may also influence the choices you make: Can you be informal in your tone, like in a blog entry about trying a new food recipe? Do you personally know the readers of a letter of recommendation you're writing for someone else? Finally, is the occasion light-hearted, or is it serious, for example a White Paper regarding sustainable energy sources in Third World countries that you hope will influence policy decision-makers?

To "I" or not to "I": Should you use the first person in your paper?

Consider these two sentences:

> In this section, I argue that a first-person tone of voice actively creates an intimate relationship with the reader.
> In this section, the argument will be made that a first-person tone of voice actively creates an intimate relationship with the reader.

The first sentence seems more intimate, doesn't it? The second is a bit impersonal, not to mention written in a *passive voice*. You may have seen an instructor's comment on your paper: "Avoid the passive voice," or, maybe just "pv" (if this is the case, hopefully you're given a key to make sense of the acronyms). In discussing the use of first-person voice, we're also going to discuss why you might want to avoid the passive voice (and why you see it being used again and again in academic journal articles). Of course, your instructor may have specific directions on whether or not you can use the first person in your paper. As long as it's not overused, as we'll talk about below, you'll likely find that most teachers don't have a problem with the use of "I." So let's talk about when and why you might want to use it.

When should I use the first-person voice?

If you're going to use the first-person voice in your paper, it's better to establish your use of it near the beginning. It doesn't have to be used in the first sentence or even the first paragraph, but somewhere in the first two paragraphs of a paper is a good rule of thumb. Why should you establish its use early on? Imagine you're reading a five-page paper peppered with phrases like "the author will argue," "this research uncovers," and "this study is intended to show..." Then, in the last paragraph you come across the sentence, "I conclude this paper with a personal example..." It's a bit jarring, isn't it?

There's nothing necessarily wrong with concluding with a personal example, and your class guidelines may not prohibit it, but in the case of this hypothetical paper, the *tone* of the last sentence is different from the tone of the rest of the paper. Up until the last paragraph, the tone of the paper was one of distanced, infallible authority, as is often the case when writers describe themselves as "the author" or "the researcher"; using these terms makes someone sound more like an objective authority and less of a fallible human to readers. The author, by referring to herself in the third person, creates a kind of "Wizard of Oz" effect by not letting the reader encounter the "I" behind the curtain. Just like the wizard in the classic American film, the author makes a series of proclamations that sound authoritative (and, therefore, likely to be thought true or credible) because the reader isn't allowed to see the human being behind the words. Of course, that authoritative tone may be the effect for which the author is striving (we'll talk more about third-person use later in the chapter), but using the third person throughout the paper makes the use of "I" at the end of the paper jarring, just as when (spoiler alert!) Toto pulls the curtain back to reveal the man who calls himself "The Wizard," and Dorothy and her friends are shocked and angry. As an author, you don't want readers to be angry with you at the end of your paper.

Our discussion so far has focused on the consistency of using the first person, not necessarily whether you should use it. So, when *should* you use "I"? The use of "I" for a class paper is usually acceptable and warranted when:

- You're writing about a topic of which you have personal experience.
- You want your paper to have a more informal tone (and your instructor okays it)

Remember, if you're planning on using "I" in your paper, you should incorporate it early on so your use at any point later isn't jarring to the reader. The *when* of using the first person is relatively easy to understand – just introduce it early in your paper and be consistent. It's the *why* that's a bit tricky.

Why should I use the first-person voice?
Most students probably have the same reasons for using the first-person voice. Consider the following, from real-life students:

- "I would use the first person in a paper in which I was writing about a personal experience. I would also use first person in a persuasive paper to show credibility."
- "I would write in first person if I am asked to write about my stance or personal opinion on a topic."
- "I would use first person to describe myself or my beliefs."

There are good intentions behind using the first person, as you can see in the students' words above, but they are *not necessarily good reasons* to use the first-person voice. While the students quoted in this section are fairly thoughtful

Table 4.1 Myths about using the first-person voice in academic papers

- MYTH #1: It's much more difficult to craft sentences without the "I." Using "I" is easy to do.
- MYTH #2: Using "I" in papers allows writers to pass off arguments as "only" opinions and makes arguments less threatening to readers.
- MYTH #3: Using an "I" in papers creates an air of authority and, therefore, makes the paper more credible.

about their use of the first person, in most cases its use is simply the result of bad habits developed over time. In my experience teaching English composition and communication, I've noticed that students have developed some misconceptions about the first person in class papers. Below, we'll examine the myths behind each of these reasons before moving on to *good* reasons for using the first person (see Table 4.1).

Let's more closely examine each of these reasons as a way of getting to the *real* reasons why you should use first person in a paper.

- MYTH #1: It's much more difficult to craft sentences without the "I." Using "I" is easy to do.

Sure, it's easy to use "I" to start sentences; we do it all the time in our conversations. We might also use "I" as a hedge, as in "I feel," "I believe," or "I think," communicating our feelings, beliefs, and opinions while also indicating an acknowledgment that these are "our" beliefs, and others are free to disagree with them. Studies indicate that women in many Western countries are particularly inclined to the use of hedges and qualifiers in face-to-face communication because of societal gender norms that often teach them to not be outspoken (Holmes 1990). Experts disagree on whether it's a good idea for women or men to use these hedges in workplace communication (Ferro 2015). Certainly, the written word is different from the spoken word, in the relationship between author/speaker and the readers/audience and in the effect words have on the readers/audience. Regardless, the use of "I" in a paper, while seemingly easy, may have a similar effect on readers.

In short, using "I" because it's easy to start sentences that way is *not* good practice, and it can also prompt readers to discount or devalue our argument. We want to be sure our readers/audience take us seriously and don't think, "Oh, it's only that author's opinion. I can take it or leave it." We want to present such a compelling argument that our readers *can't* "leave it."

Indeed, the second myth regarding the use of "I" exemplifies the thought pattern some students employ when using the first person:

- MYTH #2: Using "I" in papers allows writers to pass off arguments as "only" opinions and makes arguments less threatening to readers.

In adhering to this myth, student writers might believe the reader will give them a "pass" if tthey use the first person; they hope readers might say to themselves, well, the author uses "I" so she clearly understands this is only her opinion and I'm free to disagree with it. While we don't want to alienate our readers with our arguments (remember the invitational approach discussed in Chapter 3), we certainly don't want to come off as wishy-washy. We've done the research, we should consider ourselves "experts." Of course, we are arguing our opinions. But when making arguments stating our *opinion*, we need to support our opinions with evidence when we write; that's what makes something an *argument* as opposed to merely an *opinion*.

Nonetheless, a lot of students don't feel they have the knowledge or experience to make the sort of claims their instructors want them to make. So, to compensate, they turn to the first person, hoping their use of "I" will make them sound more knowledgeable. This third myth is actually counter to the second one we discussed:

- MYTH #3: Using an "I" in papers lends them an air of authority and, therefore, makes the paper more credible.

Holding on to this myth is understandable. In terms of academic papers, especially those written by undergraduate and graduate students, an author who distances herself from the reader by using the *third person* has a tendency to sound more authoritative (provided her reasoning is sound and the paper is well written). An op-ed piece in the *New York Times* from a well-respected politician will probably benefit from a first-person voice because she already has credibility with certain readers. But what about a student paper?

Using a first-person voice to make oneself sound more authoritative may not work. Although a student has presumably done the research required to write with some degree of authority, the student doesn't have what is called *initial credibility*, which is the trustworthiness and authority a speaker has *before* a speech – as opposed to *derived credibility*, which is credibility that a speaker gains *as a result of* giving a speech (Griffin 2011). In other words, readers may not come to the paper expecting a knowledgeable voice as they would with a piece by someone whom they already know. So, yes, you may be an expert and you may have authority, as we discussed with Myth #2, but using the first person because you think that *in and of itself* gives you credibility is a mistake.

In short, using the first person doesn't automatically give a writer credibility, nor does it lessen the chances a reader might disagree with said writer. So, how does it function for writers? *Why* should we use it? Of course, it's always best to check with your instructor for the requirements or conventions of the paper assignment. But in general, writers should use the first person for the reasons and situations listed in Table 4.2.

Table 4.2 When and why you should use the first person in academic papers

---

- You are writing a paper about your own experiences or using personal experiences as examples in your paper.
- You are writing a paper that is informal in tone and you want to create a more intimate relationship with your readers than the third person allows.
- The conventions of the research method (ethnographic, rhetorical) and paradigm in which you're writing (interpretive, critical) allow and/or encourage the use of the first person in academic essays.

Student Spotlight: Using the First Person

Let's take a look at a paragraph from an actual student paper. The co-authors for this paper wanted to study the role of communication in pickup basketball games. Since they both played pickup games regularly, they decided to observe and participate in games at the local university's recreation center. Since they're both avid basketball players, it would seem kind of silly *not* to use the first person, right? In describing their data-gathering procedures, they did, in fact, use the first person:

> While studying communication in pickup basketball, we used a few methods to collect our data. We began by doing observations in the Recreation Center (RC). For seven weeks, we went in the afternoons between 3:00 pm and 4:00 pm on Tuesdays and Thursdays and made observations. From prior experience going to the RC, we knew that this is when the RC is at its busiest. In the hour between 3:00 pm and 4:00 pm games would happen. The winning team would stay on the court, and a new team would be made up to play them. When players were sitting out, waiting to play, some players would shoot alone. The more familiar teams would sit on the side watching the game, and converse with one another. We took notes on every game and what happened in between games in our notebooks sitting courtside. Later, the notes were transcribed on our computers.

Clearly, their familiarity with the Recreation Center helped them conduct their research. In this passage, the use of the first-person "I" is based on the first and third bullet points in Table 4.2. And it reads better than if they were to write "From prior experience going to the RC, *the authors* knew that this is when the RC is at its busiest." Again, this may not be the best choice for all of your class papers, but when the assignment allows it and will enhance – not detract from – the relationship with your readers, the use of the first person may be a good choice.

Writing academic papers is difficult; this book is not trying to convince you otherwise. However, I believe such writing is difficult in part because *you haven't been and likely won't be asked to write like this in any other situation.* Teachers like to say the classroom is preparation for the real world. And when it comes to some assignments, this is probably true. But chances are, you will alter the style of writing you learn in your class to apply to the occasion, purpose, and audience for which you're writing outside of your class. The purpose of this book is not only to provide training and guidance for students to write effective class papers, it's also to provide students the tools to write well in any situation outside of the classroom. Let's not kid ourselves: academic writing has very specific conventions that don't necessary apply to other writing situations outside of the classroom (we covered some of these in Chapter 1). Using the first person because you don't know any differently will hinder you from obtaining the flexibility to write well in all situations. So, be thoughtful about *why* you're using the first person.

That said, there is a danger in *not* using the first person. Students may go so far in avoiding the first person that they lapse into the *passive voice*, something I illustrated at the beginning of this section. In all cases, save for a few writing conventions that predominate in the sciences and social sciences, students should avoid the passive voice. Why and how are two questions we will cover later in this chapter. For now, let's move on to a less frequently used but occasionally effective voice sometimes used in papers: the second person.

Second person, second choice: I'm talking to "You"

You're reading this passage thinking to yourself, "Why do I need to know all this? My papers are best when they just flow from me." You put this book aside and begin writing your paper about social media and communication: *When you see the words "social media," you expect to encounter hate, vitriol, and narcissism.* "But wait a minute," you think, "what if my reader doesn't expect to encounter these things when using social media?" By asking that question, you've just *answered* your first question about why you need know about voice when writing your papers. I began this paragraph by using "you." But perhaps you're *not* thinking "Why do I need to know all this?" By putting words into your mouth (or head) that you disagree with, I might have alienated you as a reader. As with the previous section, we'll start our discussion of the second-person voice by exploring when it might be a good idea to use the second person in a paper.

When should I use the second-person voice?
The intentions behind using the second person in a paper are usually good: an author wants to connect with his or her readers. The most obvious way to make this connection would seem to be to address them directly: "You, yes, you reading this paper, here's what I'd like you to think about..." In most cases of academic writing, there are very few occasions on which you should use the second person. In fiction, an author can get away with using "you" to put the reader in certain situations. In creative nonfiction essays written with metaphors, similes, figures or speech, imagery, and other language one might not find in an academic paper, this also holds true in terms of putting readers in certain situations. While some of the academic papers you write may be close to creative nonfiction, it's better to avoid the second person in academic papers *unless* you're absolutely sure: (a) your instructor allows it; (b) the writing conventions of the type of paper you're writing allow it; and (c) you're using it sparingly but consistently so as not to jar the reader.

Why should I use the second-person voice?
Of course, there are exceptions to every rule. And so let's examine those exceptions by looking at some reasons why you might use the second person. As with the previous section, let's begin our discussion of *why* a student should use the second person voice by discussing some *not necessarily good reasons* why students might be inclined to use it.

Student Spotlight: Bad Habits, Mindless Writing

Too often, students are *mindless* about their use of the second person and don't think about the ways it can affect the reader. Several students explained this mindlessness in written comments for one of the classes I teach:

- "I use second person often without thought."
- "Instances when I have used 'you' in my paper have happened unconsciously when writing persuasive narratives."
- "I believe that my use of second person is usually accidental."

Indeed, it's easy to imagine that most instances of the second person, a voice we don't often encounter in fiction let alone in academic writing, are usually accidental. But why, then, would students be compelled to use it? As we can see from the following student reflections, the intention behind its use is usually good. Students recounted that they used the second person in a few situations:

- "Where it sounded awkward to say 'One should…' or 'He or she…' or 'A person…'"
- "I would use the second person to give my opinion to someone. For example, 'You should…'"

So, we have two kinds of good intentions. One is to adhere to proper academic paper-writing convention. The second is to sound persuasive. I understand this mindset and certainly sympathize with it. However, there are probably other ways to accomplish what you want without using the second person.

Students, especially in writing-heavy majors like communication or rhetoric and writing studies, learn pretty quickly the conventions for academic paper-writing. And, as awkward as it may sound, one of those conventions is the use of the third person (I discuss that in more detail in the next section). Another convention quickly learned is to properly express one's opinion. As it turns out, both are ideal reasons for using the second person. In order to get to these *good* reasons, I've boiled things down to some myths about the second person: see Table 4.3.

As in the previous section, I'll address each of these myths by using some hypothetical examples. The first myth may seem a bit puzzling, as we've just discussed how using the first person is usually a way we might try to sound more credible in our writing:

- MYTH #1: The second person helps an author make his or her opinion sound more "credible."

Table 4.3 Myths about using the second-person voice in academic papers

---

- MYTH #1: The second person helps an author make his or her opinion sound more "credible."
- MYTH #2: The second person is more persuasive than the first- or third-person voice.

Why would we think the use of the second-person voice makes our opinion sound more credible? Well, it's likely because through the use of "you" we're hoping to put the reader in a particular state of mind, in which we can ask them to feel a certain way or believe a certain thing. For example, when writing a paper about the legalization of marijuana in the United States, you might write:

> You are sitting on your couch feeling like you're going to die. The drugs the doctors have given you for your cancer haven't worked. The chemotherapy is working, but it leaves you sick. The only thing that eases your pain and nausea is marijuana. But you can't have any; some politician sitting in an office somewhere is convinced it's "immoral" and something only used by stupid kids...

By putting the reader in the shoes of this cancer patient, you obviously hope the reader will gain some empathy and therefore come to believe – or perhaps even more strongly believe – that marijuana should be legalized.

Does this use of the second person make you, the author, more credible? Ironically, attempting to put the reader in the position of this cancer sufferer does nothing to increase your credibility. The reader doesn't get a sense of how much you know about cancer or even get an idea of your arguments for legalization (beside a medical reason). This is solely an emotional appeal, and one that may be too jarring to affect the reader in the way you want.

I address what I mean by "jarring" by unpacking the second myth about using the second person:

- MYTH #2: The second person is more persuasive than the first- or third-person voice.

In the first example, you obviously want to be persuasive, attempting to convince the reader that the legalization – or at least the medicalization – of marijuana in the United States is something that should be instituted (a claim of policy, as we discussed in Chapter 3). While the use of the second person doesn't make you more credible, is it at least persuasive enough to put the reader in the position of someone suffering from cancer? The answer, as with the first myth about using the second person, is no.

First, the use of the second person can have a jarring effect. And while there are occasions on which an author may want to make the reader feel uncomfortable, those occasions normally don't arise in an academic class paper. For example, if you really want a reader to feel the shame, humiliation, and violation of bullying, you may relate a story about when you were bullied. This may generate a reader's sympathy for you the author and may pull them into the story. This would, of course, require you to write in the first person and use "I." Using "you" in this story may, indeed, put them in the middle of a bullying scenario, but the reader may not want to be there. And while you may say, "Well, I want the reader to feel the discomfort of bullying," consider whether that reader is likely to continue to follow you through a review of the scholarly literature about bullying after feeling that uncomfortable. Using the first person to describe your own discomfort may

Table 4.4 When and why you should use the second person in academic papers

- You want to directly address the reader in a paper that is informal in tone.
- You foreshadow its use and place the reader in a non-threatening situation or scene.

not only garner you sympathy and engagement from the reader, it may also bolster your credibility as an expert on that particular topic. Further, if the use of "you" isn't established early, in the first page or so, the reader may be jarred in a different but still substantive way.

Second, the use of "you" may not only be jarring to the reader but can distance you the author from the reader. Using "you" forces the reader to put him or herself in the position you are suggesting: "You walk up to a kid in the junior high hallway and push him against the locker." The reader may not want to be the bully in that scenario, and, as a result, may stop reading or, worse, grow to dislike you because you've made them a mean bully. You've also transported the reader back to their awkward pre-teen years, a place no reader probably wants to revisit! And when a reader dislikes the author or is upset with the author, especially if that reader is someone tasked with evaluating your paper, the outcome may not be to your liking. Such animosity toward an author may be fine if you're writing fiction, but for an academic paper? Not so much.

So when is it a good idea to use the second person in an academic paper, if it ever is? Table 4.4 addresses this. As you can see, there aren't many situations in which using the second person in an academic paper is desirable. One option that might be permissible (always check with your instructor) is that you want to address the reader directly in a paper that's already informal in tone. The problem is, most of the academic papers you will write will probably *not* be that informal. Additionally, you can foreshadow its use and try to make it less jarring for the reader by easing them into the second person. For example, writing "Imagine yourself..." rather than simply starting a sentence with "You." Unfortunately, this probably won't prevent your reader from resisting a situation in which he or she doesn't want to be (try it on yourself – complete the phrase "Imagine yourself..." with the place, person, or situation you absolutely want nothing to do with. Does that phrase make the scenario any less repulsive to you?).

To sum up, there's probably no reason to use the second person in your papers. That I have used "you" through this section and chapter isn't lost on me; I understand that by using "you" I'm putting you in certain situations and scenarios, *making* you commit certain writing errors, ones of which you may otherwise not be guilty. Consider the effect my use of "you" has had on you the reader, and think twice the next time you use it.

Convention and confusion: When to use the third person in your paper

To transition from second-person to third-person voice, let's consider a sentence from an actual student paper. This author wrote about her experiences competing as a female bodybuilder. In one section of her literature review, she explains that, unlike other team sports in which athletes directly interact with each other on the field, pitch, or court, bodybuilding forces the athlete to exert personal control over their own body:

> In competitive bodybuilding, there is no body to be manipulated other than one's own. Hence, one is arguably more focused on personal control.

Notice the use of the third person in this sentence ("one's own..."). While it may sound a bit awkward, the logical alternative would be to use the second person, so that the sentence reads: "...there is no body to be manipulated other than your own. Hence, you are arguably more focused..." While this may sound more conversational, competitive bodybuilding is probably a situation most of us are unfamiliar with. So putting us in this situation, I argue, doesn't do much to enhance our understanding of it.

So, the logical alternative to the second person, and even to the first person, is the third person, right? Well, yes and no. He, She, It, One are all variants of the third person, and we're all familiar with the third person in academic papers. The infamous, awkward phrasing of "When one examines the data, one can see..." is commonplace in many social science articles. This is the most common voice in academic papers for a variety of reasons. For scholars, these reasons have to do with the conventions of reporting social science research. But before we get to those, let's take a look at the reasons some students gave me for using the third person in their paper:

- "I feel it is the most intelligent form of writing."
- "It makes the paper feel professional and scholarly, and also helps to keep it ambiguous enough to apply to a range of readers."
- "I've been taught [third person] is a more credible way of writing."
- "It's a way to disconnect my opinions from the paper."

One common sentiment in the above student responses is that the third person is usually considered to be the most credible form of writing. That may be true, but as we'll find out, only in certain situations. In this section, we'll again discuss when you should consider using the third person, why you might use the third person, and some myths and realities behind using the third person.

When should I use the third-person voice?

As one student noted, the third person is the "academic paper default." Indeed, if no other parameters of the paper assignment are specified, the third person is probably the safest bet for several reasons. The third person follows academic conventions. Most of the published social science research you'll read in disciplines like communication, sociology, anthropology, and psychology, and often in the humanities disciplines (literature, history, political science), will use the third person. So, there is some truth to the notion of "academic default."

Another occasion on which the third person might provide useful is when you are writing about a controversial issue in which you wish to portray all sides with equal weight and valence. Granted, a first-person narrative of your personal experience regarding the loss of a family member due to health-care problems

Table 4.5 Myths about using the third-person voice in academic papers

- MYTH #1: The third person is boring, impersonal, and too formal.
- MYTH #2: The third person gives the author credibility.
- MYTH #3: All instructors prefer that students write in the third person.

might be a powerful way in which to argue for changes in the health-care system. But if you're looking to inform your readers more than persuade them about an issue, the third person is probably a better choice. While you're not disconnecting your "opinions from the paper," as one student explained, you *are* distancing yourself from the issue and thereby providing a more balanced feel to your essay.

Why should I use the third-person voice?

The occasions on which you might choose to write in the third person are, of course, related to the reasons why you might choose to use the third person. As with the previous two sections, let's take a look at the myths many students have about the third person, summarized in Table 4.5.

As with using the first- and second-person voice, these myths are certainly rooted in some degree of accuracy. Take the first myth:

- MYTH #1: The third person is boring, impersonal, and too formal.

This is commonly believed among students, in large part because students may not be excited or engaged by academic essays, at least as undergraduates just beginning to explore scholarly research. And, granted, the third person, with its "one would argue…" sentence structure, does sound a little stilted and awkward. But using the third person doesn't necessarily mean the writing itself is boring. Even though a student is writing in the third person, she can still use figures of speech and imagery, two vital components of engaging writing.

The second myth is also understandable:

- MYTH #2: The third person gives the author credibility.

In other words, many students believe that by separating oneself from one's opinions through the third person, they will seem less biased and therefore more credible. What's interesting is that, if you recall, people also believe that using the first person increases credibility. So, which is it? Well – both. And neither. An author's credibility doesn't solely rest on whether she is using the first- or third-person voice. Credibility in academic papers comes from supporting one's argument using evidence in the form of research and vivid examples, and citing sources (among other things addressed elsewhere in this book).

So, why do all teachers want you to write in the third person? Or do they?

- MYTH #3: All instructors prefer that students write in the third person.

This third myth is perhaps closest to the truth among the three myths about writing in the third person. While it's true that the third person is the convention with academic papers, it's not always true that your instructors prefer you write in the third person. While it's best to check with your instructor, let your topic guide you. A story about a personal experience would obviously be best written

Table 4.6 When and why you should use the third person in academic papers

- You are writing a conventional academic paper and your instructor provides no additional guidance in terms of style.
- You are reporting the results of an original quantitative research paper that employs survey data and/or data gathered from experimental methods.

in the first person. A balanced, informative paper about a controversial issue might be best written in the third person. A persuasive essay could be either, or a mix of voices that uses a personal example written in the first person but otherwise is written in the third person. Table 4.6 lays out the when and why of using the third person in academic papers. Since the third person is the "default" voice in academic writing, we only need a few reasons that cover a wide variety of writing situations you're likely to encounter in your paper.

The major obstacle is knowing when to bring the author (you) to the foreground and when to remain unobtrusive. Remember that it will seem weird to readers to encounter "I think…" at one point in your paper, and then later in the paper to come across the phrase "The author believes…" Be consistent. That is the rule of thumb regardless of the voice in which you write. One danger in deciding what voice to use is that you become so cautious that you lapse into the passive voice.

Actively avoiding the passive voice

You may have seen the comments in the margins of your paper: "Passive voice" or the abbreviation "pv." I was surprised to find out that many students go through their entire academic career never really knowing what it means. After you've read this section, I hope you'll better understand what this is and why you should avoid it. To put it simply, the passive voice is passive because no one or thing is *doing the action*. If a sentence reads "I argue that a first-person tone of voice creates an intimate relationship with the reader," there is a person doing the arguing. You know this because the author refers to him or herself (assuming we don't know the identified gender of the author). This sentence is written in an *active voice*. Such a sentence could also begin: "This section argues…." Although we know someone wrote the section, the section is the thing doing the action, in this case, the arguing.

But who is doing the arguing in the following sentence: "In this section, the argument will be made that a first-person tone of voice creates an intimate relationship with the reader"? We can assume the author is making the argument; who else would it be? Why then, you may ask, doesn't the author just write "I argue"? And why, you may also ask, does my teacher insist that we don't use "I" in our papers? Chances are your instructor, like the author in the previously quoted sentence, is following stylistic conventions commonly associated with social science research papers. As with the previous section, we'll further explore this topic by asking why some authors might use the passive voice, why we should usually avoid using the passive voice, and how we can avoid using the passive voice.

Why do people use the passive voice?

For as much as you may hear writing instructors, critics, bloggers, and anyone else with an opinion on writing say it, the passive voice is not only fairly common (among certain types of writing) but encouraged – or at least, not *dis*couraged. In fact, you may read a lot of published academic articles in your classes that are written in the passive voice, and you may be rewarded for writing the same way. Why is this? And if this is the case, why would I spend a whole section of this chapter on avoiding the passive voice?

There are many reasons why someone might use the passive voice in writing. Some think it sounds more "scholarly." Some students, used to reading research articles from communication studies and other related disciplines, may have mindlessly adopted the writing style. Regardless of the reasons why people use the passive voice, there are just as many, even more compelling, reasons why people should avoid using the passive voice. I will detail some reasons why you should avoid using the passive voice and how you can do that.

Why should we avoid the passive voice?

What's so bad about the passive voice, anyway? What difference does it make? Classes will be attended. Papers will be written. The class paper that is written the best will receive the best grade either way. Papers that are graded fairly will be justly rewarded. The class that is taught most effectively will produce good papers.

Well, not exactly. The sentences in the previous paragraph were written to illustrate how awkward the passive voice sounds. Or, to put it in an *active voice*, I wrote the above sentences in the passive voice to illustrate how awkward the passive voice sounds. But the passive voice still might be difficult to understand. Let's start with a simpler example. We all know the joke that starts, "Why did the chicken cross the road?" Let's change that question into a declarative sentence in the passive voice:

The road was crossed by the chicken.

Note that, although the chicken (the subject) is doing the action (crossing), there is no action verb. Normally in the English language, the subject would appear in the sentence first, then the verb, then the object, as in this simple sentence:

The boy kicked the ball.

You can locate the subject, verb, and object, right? The boy (subject) kicked (verb) the ball (object). How would this read in the passive voice?

The ball was kicked by the boy.

Notice how the ball has now taken the grammatical position of the subject. Not only is that inaccurate (the ball is the object, not the subject), but it tends to read and sound (when read aloud) awkward. Again, this is a convention of academic writing you may find in many published research articles in the social sciences.

My point here is not to denigrate the academic writing that uses the passive voice, but to help you think more mindfully about your writing choices. Being mindful about using the passive voice is half the solution to this problem; avoiding it is the other half. Should you wish to stop at the first half and simply tell yourself, "I know I'm using the passive voice, but this is a convention of the type of writing I'm doing," you're at least being mindful about the choice. But avoiding the passive voice whenever you can makes for even better writing. The next section provides some ways to help you avoid the passive voice.

Don't be a writing zombie: How to avoid using the passive voice

What do zombies and the passive voice have in common? Well, besides the fact that zombies, as they are most often depicted in movies and on television, seem to be mindlessly lumbering toward an unspecified destination (unless there are humans to attack), you can also use the concept of zombies to identify the passive voice. This trick is generally attributed to Rebecca Johnson (2012), Assistant Professor of National Security Affairs at the Command and Staff College at Marine Corps University. To test her students' sentences, she explained on Twitter, she asked if they could insert "by zombies" after the verb. If the sentence made grammatical sense, it showed the sentence was written in the passive voice. For example, "Experts advise us to avoid the passive voice" is written in the *active* voice. "It has been advised to avoid the passive voice" can be changed to "It has been advised **by zombies** to avoid the passive voice." And voilà! You have just exposed in this latter sentence the zombified passive voice.

Since, as we previously covered, your thoughts and opinions form the basis for your arguments, it's important to be mindful of which voice you're using. The social science disciplines (some areas of communication, psychology, and sociology, for example) have conventions for the use of voice. Likewise, disciplines more closely aligned with the humanities (including some areas of communication, history, and literature) have their own writing conventions. We'll cover many of these conventions, especially for communication and related social science disciplines, when we go over common types of assignments in later chapters. For now, let's concentrate on focusing your arguments into a thesis sentence.

Thesis Sentences

Thesis sentences are the main point of your paper encapsulated in, of course, a sentence. Before we go over what a thesis sentence should do, let's talk briefly about what it isn't. Importantly, thesis sentences are *not* simply previews of the main points of your paper. Previews are important, as I discuss later on, but if the argument for your paper is "Below, I cover the following reasons why gun control rhetoric in the US is divisive," then you should be rethinking your argument. Chances are, though, that such a sentence isn't the main point of your paper. If you don't already know what the main point of your paper is, some thoughtful reflection can help.

Thesis sentences should be specific. For example, a paper about the inflammatory nature of gun-control rhetoric in the United States might include the following thesis: "The rhetoric surrounding the issue of gun control in the United States is divisive." Well, anyone who pays attention to the news coming out of the United States can probably guess this is the case. Now, this doesn't mean you can't analyze the rhetoric on all sides of the issue. But you should probably be a bit more specific so that your audience knows they can expect some new insight from your paper. You might revise that thesis to: "The rhetoric on all sides of the gun-control issue in the United States serves to move all parties involved further and further from any common ground, making consensus seem impossible." Note some of the changes made to its specificity. The reader is now aware that you are conceptualizing more than two sides to this controversy, and the reader gets some sense of your takeaway (the rhetoric has a negative effect on all sides achieving common ground). Of course, it's still broad in the sense that we don't get any specific analysis, but that's okay; it's more specific than the initial version and sets up the argument well.

Once you have a thesis sentence, you've established the foundation for the rest of the paper. But there's a big difference between establishing a foundation and building on it. One of main critiques I hear from students about their own papers and about reading other students' papers has to do with "flow," as in "This paper flows well" or "This paper didn't flow well." And when I ask them about it, they're always hard pressed to explain what "flow" means, or how they can tell when a paper "flows" or doesn't "flow." This concept is definitely important, however, and I explore it in the next section.

Does the Paper "Flow"? What Does That Even Mean?

This concept of "flow" is sometimes easy to notice in a paper, but often difficult to define. I am conceptualizing it here as *the ease or difficulty with which an audience reads and comprehends your paper*. Now, you may think that your ultimate goal is to make it as easy as possible for an audience to read and comprehend what you've written. Well, yes and no. There may be times when you want your paper to be smooth and times when you want it to be a little rougher or more abrupt. Sometimes you want your audience to *work* to understand something. What do I mean by this? I cover below several factors that contribute to the "flow" of your paper.

The first factor students often don't consider is **a mix of short and long sentences**. Some sentences are long, including modifying phrases such as definitions or caveats to an accepted definition, and may span several typed lines in your paper. Some sentences are short. Notice my previous two sentences, the first long and the second shorter. Mixing long and short sentences creates a pleasing aesthetic effect in your paper. You may think that short sentences are easy to understand and digest. So, wouldn't it be good to have all short sentences in your paper, as long you're citing evidence and making an argument?

Imagine if all your sentences were short. Each paragraph consists of short sentences. Imagine this again and again. Every paragraph of your paper has sentences no longer than one line. Your paper would be dotted with periods. Those periods cause the reader to stop reading. The effect can be abrupt. The effect can be halting. Reading your paper might be like hitting the brakes intermittently as you drive. Your passenger would get annoyed. And the reader may get annoyed reading your paper.

Notice that there wasn't one comma in the previous paragraph. How did you feel reading it? Chances are it felt a little like someone hitting the brakes on a bus or car or bicycle every 10 seconds as they drove. As a passenger (or driver), you'd probably feel jostled and uncomfortable. Do you want your reader to feel this way? Probably not. At least, not for your *entire* paper. There may be a reason why you want them to stop abruptly. Maybe you want them to digest a surprising fact. It might be important that they think about the previous sentence. Whatever the reason, it's important to mindful about your mix of long and short sentences.

One method you should *not* use to make your sentences long is to insert big words just for the sake of having big words in a sentence. **Word choice** is an important aspect of the "flow" of your paper. Let's run that last sentence through a thesaurus and see what we get: "Locution preference is a paramount facet of the progress of your treatise." Which sounds better? Which is easier to read? Which is easier to understand? You may have read a paper by a student – or you may have been that student – who seems to keep a thesaurus at their side when writing. There's no reason to make your words needlessly complicated. You don't want to use big words just for the sake of sounding smart. So, keeping it simple is the second aspect of how to control the ease or difficulty with which audiences read your papers.

While you should avoid using a thesaurus for every other word in your paper, you definitely want to vary your wording so as not to be repetitive. Some words important to your area of study shouldn't be changed. For example, if you're writing a paper about romantic relationships, then you know there's a plethora of scholarly research about romantic relationships. It's difficult to use a synonym for romantic relationships and stay faithful to that area of research; "relationships" is too broad, as it could cover friendship and family, among other things. "Affair," "liaison," and "marriage" are all types of relationships, but they aren't accurate replacements in terms of the scholarly literature. However, other words not specific to that area of research should be changed up every so often. For example, "study," as in the study of relationships, can also be the "examination" or "investigation" of relationships.

The final way to help the "flow" of your paper, or to make it easier for your audience to read, is to **avoid filler**. Most students are familiar with "filler": the sentences that don't add a whole lot to the paper but are added just to get the word or page count up to the minimum requirements of your teacher. Readers (and instructors!) can tell filler from the more substantial parts your writing. Thinking back to our discussion about argument (claim, support, warrant) in Chapter 3 should help you avoid filler by prompting you to fully support your claims. I provide another strategy to help you with the flow of the paper and avoiding filler in the form below.

The TESLA Method: Transmitting Ideas Smoothly and Effortlessly

Nikola Tesla was a groundbreaking inventor who is credited with, among many things, finding a method of energy conduction that was seemingly effortless. I'd like you to consider that idea as I introduce the TESLA method as a way of transmitting ideas smoothly.

The TESLA Method of paragraph construction

1) **T**opic sentence that previews the content of the paragraph for the reader, then...
2) **E**xplain and evaluate past research, and in doing so provide...
3) **S**upport for your topic sentence and overall thesis or argument, after which...
4) **L**ink back to your topic sentence by offering a mini wrap-up of the paragraph,
5) **A**nd... [continue in any number of ways, including transitioning to the next paragraph or sentence]

The first step is to write your *topic sentence*. A topic sentence is basically a thesis sentence for a particular paragraph and usually appears as the first or second sentence in that paragraph. In fact, your topic sentence should be directly linked to the thesis or *claim* of your paper, functioning as a backing statement for the thesis of your paper. And just as a thesis sentence gives readers the main point of your paper, a topic sentence offers readers the main point of your paragraph. This is why you'll want to think twice about citing research in your topic sentence. Granted, citing research in the first sentence of a paragraph is something you often see in published articles. But remember, just because you see it in print doesn't mean it's an effective writing practice. Additionally, citing research in the first sentence of a paragraph can be considered a writing convention of a particular paradigm of research, just like using the passive voice.

Write Away

To ensure your topic sentences provide support to your thesis sentence, try this trick:

1) Place your thesis sentence at the top of a blank sheet in a new document. You can do this on paper or on a computer.
2) Write or cut and paste each topic sentence of your paper below the thesis sentence.
3) Read these statements through, asking if they make sense, both logically and grammatically.
4) Revise as needed, then cut and paste back into your paper.
5) Revise the paragraphs for each topic sentence to make sure you support your thesis sentence.

Next, you *explain and evaluate past research*. Explaining research is fairly straightforward; it's probably what you're used to doing when writing a literature review. Evaluating research, however, might be different from what you normally do. It simply means to assess the relative worth of this research with regards to your topic sentence. In short, does this research support your topic sentence? If so, how? This should be done with a little more artistry than simply stating, "This research supports my topic sentence because..." While we are building a house upon the foundation of topic sentences, remember that people often want their houses to look aesthetically pleasing in addition to being solid. Drawing attention to the foundation you're building (i.e., literally writing "This research supports my argument...") is akin to leaving the pipes and wires for your house exposed to passersby.

   In explaining and evaluating past research, you will also *support your own argument*. This means that you'll make sure readers understand how the research you cite supports both your topic sentences and your thesis. Always ask yourself, how does this explanation support my claim? And don't forget our discussion of *warrants* in Chapter 3. What is *implied* by your citing the research you do? If you're citing a personal website, the warrant connecting your support and claim is that your topic can be easily understood and evaluated by a layperson (someone not in an academic field or classroom). Is that really what you want to communicate to readers? That your topic can be researched by almost anyone, regardless of their educational level? While this may be true of some of the concepts you're dealing with, part of the reason you're getting your degree is so that you can *translate* academic research *for* other people to put into practice. But if others are already doing this on their personal website, why bother even getting your degree? Obviously, I'm not advocating that you drop out of school. Instead, I'm reminding you to pay attention to the warrants in your argument, as *whom* you cite and the *type of research* you cite communicates just as much as the content itself.

After you've fashioned each topic sentence, explained and evaluated research, and supported your argument, you have two steps remaining. First, in each paragraph you should *link back to your topic sentence.* This only requires a sentence or two to remind readers of the purpose of your paragraph. Once you're done with that, you *transition to the next paragraph, idea, point,* or *sub point.* Again, the transition only needs to be one or two sentences long. The purpose of these last two steps, as you have probably gathered by now, is to help the reader follow your argument. And it's *especially* these last two steps that will help you avoid filler in the papers you write.

Too often, student writers are so focused on the word or page count of a paper they lose track of the arguments they're making. Using the TESLA method will ensure you never have to use filler or "fluff" in your papers. Notice that, as long as you're adequately explaining and evaluating research, the type of writing you end up doing more of is not the difficult work of employing additional citations. Instead, the additional writing you're doing is relatively easy: adding *structural statements* designed to help the reader follow along. And these statements that provide structure to your paper are definitely not filler or fluff. In fact, your instructor is more likely to see them as parts of effective writing, which they are. So, following the TESLA method will help you avoid filler, provide structure to your paper, and ensure your argument is clear and clearly supported throughout your paper.

Student Spotlight: The TESLA Method

This excerpt from an undergraduate student, Katie, illustrates how the TESLA method can help you lengthen your paragraphs (and, subsequently, paper) without the use of filler, and simultaneously ensure you're providing detailed support for your topic sentence and claim. I've annotated each part of the method in italics below.

> Not only is recess favored by students, but it has also proved in studies to be beneficial to children's cognitive skills, physical health, and social-emotional skills. [*Topic sentence. Note that no research is cited.*] In an article published in *Young Children*, the author gives a summary of the benefits of recess that have been found in research studies: "Children are less fidgety and more on task when they have recess" (Jarrett, 2009, p. 67). Physical activity, which takes place during recess, has been shown to have a relationship with the development of brain connections. Jarrett (2009) argues that research has shown that the brain actually performs better with memory and attention when learning is spaced out. During playtime, children are able to learn skills such as turn-taking, sharing, teaching others, resolving issues and communicating with one another. Communicating with other peers at recess allows children to practice their social skills and learn how to develop relationships with others through their communication (Gable, 2009). Gable (2009) concludes that children do not necessarily repeat or transfer their knowledge from the interactions they have with caregivers, over to their interactions with other children. [*These six sentences*

serve to explain and evaluate *research. Notice that the student author explains each study in a way that supports her topic sentence; in short, she clarifies how recess is beneficial to children's well-being*] Therefore, recess allows young children the opportunity to learn and practice their interactions and communication skills with other children their own age. [*This sentence links back to her topic sentence. She doesn't explicitly say so, but the "Therefore" provides a sense of conclusion.*] By developing these skills at a young age, children are more likely to master them over the years, thus profiting their social abilities into adulthood. Overall, the outcome of recess proves to be a necessary and beneficial part of our children's school day. [*And summation of the paragraph that prepares the reader for the next paragraph.*]

While this author's paragraph is taken from the literature review portion of an empirical research paper about gender differences in children's communication at recess, the TESLA method will work well when explaining the methods for a research study, outlining the analysis, or constructing the conclusion portion of a paper. It will also work with any of the assignments covered in the subsequent chapters.

Paragraphs

One question I get from students a lot is "How long should a paragraph be?" First, by following the TESLA method above, you'll ensure your paragraphs are *long enough* to provide support for your thesis. But to avoid giving a typical instructor answer like, "The paragraphs should be as long as they need to be" (don't you hate it when your teacher says this?), I will provide some estimates. Unless you're writing dialogue between people for a nonfiction paper, narrative, or another assignment in which you're allowed to write in a personal voice, most writing experts (Purdue Owl 2015) agree that paragraphs should ideally be three to five sentences long, with two to three paragraphs per double-spaced, typewritten page. And there is some reasoning behind this length. First, each paragraph should have one main idea. In the Student Spotlight above, the main idea of the paragraph is the benefit of recess for child development. Remember that each Arabic numeral in an outline should consist of one main idea, as we covered in Chapter 3. Any more than that, and you should break it up into two points. It's the same idea with paragraphs. There's no reason to address more than one main idea in a paragraph, since providing support and explanation for more than one idea is essentially what you're doing for the *entire paper*.

Second, readers tend to skip longer paragraphs. The white space in a paper can be used strategically to help readers digest your ideas. This doesn't mean you should have insanely large margins or a larger font (two tricks many students employ to increase page length). What it does mean, however, is that the paragraph indents, just like periods and commas, provide a bit of a rest for readers. Think about it: what would look more appealing and readable to you, a solid page of text or a page broken up into two or three paragraphs? Always try to put yourself in the place of the reader when constructing paragraphs.

Transitions

One thing you'll realize by putting yourself in the reader's place is the benefit of transitions. We tend to think that because we're writing a paper and readers have the pages in front of them or on the screen, we don't need transitions as we might in a speech or presentation. But, just as transitions help readers follow us in a presentation, they also provide structure to our paper and help readers follow our ideas.

There are two functions of a transition: a **review** and a **preview**. The first is to provide some kind of brief summation or review of the paragraph. Since we're not talking about a review of your entire paper, which would come in the conclusion, you don't have to include everything you've discussed up to that point. A simple nod to the main idea you've covered is fine. The second is, obviously, to preview or foreshadow the coming paragraphs and ideas. Again, between paragraphs this need only be a one-sentence preview. The most artistic transitions will review and preview in the same sentence. In the previously cited student paper on gender differences in children's communication, Katie provides an effective transition (in italics):

> A difference in communication styles can also be seen when dealing with conflict. Often, the purpose of conversation for women is to develop an intimate bond with one another. Women speak about their problems and issues in a more expressive and polite manner, therefore often avoiding conflict. With men, dominance is exerted through communication, thus making conflict potentially more comfortable and more possible for them (Merchant, 2012). Tannen (2007) agrees that men are more likely to engage in verbal conflict than women are. She explains that men see life as a contest and are ready to fire back when given the chance to. *Besides engaging in dissimilar types of talk and dealing with verbal conflict differently, both men and women often times shift their communication styles during social encounters.*
>
> In Communication Accommodation Theory, people have choices on how far or how little they will accommodate someone else's speech. They can either use convergence, divergence, or overaccommodation.

The shift in communication styles is the focus of the theory she cites in the second paragraph: Communication Accommodation Theory (CAT) (Giles, Coupland, and Coupland 1991). She effectively sums up the paragraph by writing "Besides engaging in dissimilar types of talk..." (the paragraph is about differences in conflict communication), and then previews the discussion of CAT by mentioning how men and women shift their communication styles.

Figures of Speech and Other Stylistic Choices

Besides using transitions to move readers from one point to the next, there are other stylistic choices you can use to enhance the flow of your paper, or influence *the ease or difficulty with which an audience reads and comprehends* it. Parallelism, alliteration, metaphor, and imagery are all techniques you can use to make sure readers comprehend your paper. **Parallelism** is simply making sure you address items in the order in which you previewed them. For example, you may have a topic sentence that reads, "Organizational culture consists of rules, roles, and rituals." In your subsequent paragraphs, you should explain each concept in the order in which you previewed them, first unpacking what you mean by rules, then roles, then rituals. This sample topic sentence about organizational culture also has a handy device to make these three things stick in the reader's mind: **alliteration**: all three words begin with "r." Alliteration can help readers remember your point.

Although you might think **metaphor**, comparing two unlike things (sometimes using "like" or "as," which is called a **simile**), is something better suited to poetry or fiction, it can also be used to great effect in any kind of research or critical analysis paper. Let's say part of your argument is that the current research on a particular topic is incomplete and hampers us from fully understanding a certain phenomenon. You could write a sentence that reads exactly like that. But you could also use metaphor to make this problem even clearer: "The research on [your topic] is like a puzzle missing a few crucial pieces. Without more research, we will never get the whole picture." It's not like you're writing a poem in the middle of your paper: you're using a metaphor comparing research to an incomplete puzzle to create an image in your reader's mind, an image that makes your argument a little clearer.

And just as metaphor can solidify your argument for readers, **imagery** can do the same. Creating a picture for readers, similar to our puzzle metaphor in the previous paragraph, can sometimes communicate your message better than a simple declarative sentence. Imagery might be most useful in a qualitative research project in which you're required to use observations as part of your data. Likewise, you may describe an artifact like a statue or a communication ritual in an organization using imagery. For example, two students studying communication among recreational rock climbers included the following observation to illustrate how climbers work together to solve problems:

> A woman and a man are engaging in conversation about a climb, and deciding what moves a guy on the wall should make. As a man in brown corduroy pants tries a boulder route, two men stand behind him together with their hands on their hips, and look to be studying him.

This picture created by these two student authors says more to readers than, "People talk and observe each other at rock climbing gyms."

Parallelism, alliteration, metaphor, and imagery are all techniques that can enhance the readability of your paper. Of course, your entire paper doesn't have to be made up of these writing techniques. Along with mixing long and short sentences, not using big words just for the sake of sounding smart, and incorporating the TESLA method, these literary techniques can be used sparingly and still enhance the flow of your paper. In addition to these positive practices, there are some potentially distracting practices that can detract from the flow of your paper.

Grammar Reminders

Grammar is important to writing, obviously. And yet we don't pay a lot of attention to it, perhaps assuming that we've all mastered that topic back in primary or elementary school. My purpose in revisiting this subject here is not to provide a list of dos and don'ts, but instead to offer a few simple reminders. I subscribe to the school of thought that if you concentrate on making your message clear to readers, correct grammar will usually follow. Certainly, conventions of writing often dictate "proper" grammar, but even those rules are changing. Of course, grammar varies depending on the language in which one is writing. I'm going to focus on English grammar in this section.

You may have already noticed that some of the sentences in these chapters have ended in **prepositions**, such as *to*, *for*, and *with*. Opinion has drastically changed on whether it's okay to end a sentence with preposition, and the reasons have to do with clarity. For example, imagine you're walking down the street with a friend. She suddenly stops, then picks up her foot to look at the bottom of her shoe and swears under breath. You'd probably ask her, "What did you step on?" Ending that question in a preposition seems natural. But if you were to follow the grammar rule that admonishes us to never end sentences in a preposition, you would ask your friend "On what did you step?" Your friend might look at you in a funny way and wonder why you're talking like you're from the 19th century. In short, the first way of asking the question is clearer, even though it ends in a preposition. Unless your instructor expressly forbids it, you should likewise value clarity above increasingly outdated grammar rules, *unless* violating those rules gives your paper an inappropriately unprofessional or informal tone.

Indeed, **word choice** is one trouble spot for student writers, as some choices can make their papers sound too informal and, therefore, not appropriately scholarly. Remember the audience for whom you're writing; a paper for an audience of researchers and scholars (even if they are your classmates) will differ from a paper for an audience of laypeople. Nonetheless, some student writers make word choices that not only *sound* too informal but also make their point less clear. Below is a list of common word choices that often make a writer's point less clear:

- "Huge," as in "This is a *huge* problem in today's society." This word is too vague. The reader isn't sure exactly how big the problem is. Better to use statistics or more descriptive language.
- "Based off of," as in "This study is based off of existing research on relational conflict." Not only is the preposition "of" not needed here, but there are simply too many words. The phrase "based on" will suffice.
- "Into play," as in "This is where the idea of competing goals in a relationship comes into play." What does "come into play" mean here? It sounds as if the author is arguing that one thing (competing goals) affects something else, but the phrase "comes into play" makes that relationship murky.
- "Oftentimes," as in "Oftentimes, we seek to resolve conflict after it has occurred rather than manage it as it occurs." While "oftentimes" isn't incorrect per se, it's unnecessary as "often" means the same thing and is more to the point.

The phrases included here are primarily present in U.S. student writing. However, some common phrases used needlessly by U.S. students may be common and actually preferred elsewhere. For example, there's little difference between among and amongst, but "amongst" is more common among UK, Canadian, and other British English-speaking students. So, remember that in addition to writing conventions within particular paradigms and methodologies, cultural conventions may also play a part in word choice.

Another tricky part of grammar use is **subject–verb agreement**. Simply, this is matching the subject of your sentence – the person or thing doing something – with the verb – the thing being done. A common mistake I see in student papers is pairing a plural pronoun (they, some, everybody) with a singular verb, and vice versa. For example, "Some authors [plural] has [singular] concluded that..." I understand that a simple sentence like this makes this rule seem too basic to even mention in a college-level textbook. But the reason this pops up in so many student papers is because the more complex the sentence (citing multiple authors, keeping your claim, support, and evidence aligned), the easier it is to lose track of this simple rule. Consider the following sentence:

> Some of the research on doctor–patient communication in U.S. hospitals *has/have* concluded that nonverbal expressions *is/are* crucial to communicating empathy.

Which of the above pairings is correct? In the first instance, we might think *have* is correct because "hospitals" is plural. But read the sentence again. What is doing the concluding? Not the hospitals, but the *research*. So, would we write "Research have..." or "Research has..."? We would write the latter. For the second pairing, what is crucial to empathy? Expressions. We would write "Expressions are..." Rewriting this sentence, then, with the correct pairings, it would read as shown in Figure 4.2. Note the pairing of the subject and verb in each instance.

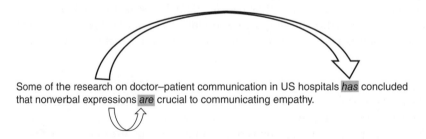

Some of the research on doctor–patient communication in US hospitals has concluded that nonverbal expressions are crucial to communicating empathy.

Figure 4.2 Subject–verb agreement

Write Away

When *proofreading* your paper, break some sentences down into a simple subject–verb pairing to make sure your grammar is correct. And remember, you should be most concerned with the clarity of your sentences and getting you message across to your readers; if you focus on that, correct grammar should follow.

Since the English language doesn't have a gender-neutral singular **pronoun**, deciding when to use "he or she" and "they" can also give writers some problems. There is a lot of debate about which pronouns to use, and if a plural pronoun is more appropriate (Nunn 2015; Petrow 2014). Of course, we want to avoid sexist language, always using "he" as a pronoun when the gender of the person in question could be something other than a "he." You may have noticed that, up to this point in the book, I often give a hypothetical example of an instructor or student and use "he" and "she" interchangeably.

But in attempting to avoid sexist language, some students may use a plural pronoun as a kind of "catch-all." For example, a student may write: "The driver was still suffering the effects of their medication, and they lost control of the car." Some argue that this use of pronouns is more inclusive of the spectrum of gender identities in our society today. Since there was only one person driving, others might argue that we really can't use "they" as the pronoun. Regardless of which side you take in this argument, the best course of action is to check with your instructor. Chances are, if you can provide your teacher with an argument as to why you might use "they" as a singular pronoun, your teacher will, at the least, thoughtfully consider your reasons. Then, if you decide to use it knowing your teacher still believes its use is grammatically incorrect, you will not be surprised if you get marked down for it in a paper. But your teacher may not have even considered the possibility of using "they," and you can begin a fruitful dialogue about grammar and gender in class papers.

Chapter Summary

This chapter has covered a lot, from when to use first-, second-, and third-person voice, to thesis and topic sentences, to how to avoid filler by using the TESLA Method for paragraphs, to common grammar issues. While all of this may be overwhelming when writing your paper, remember the guidelines for writing your papers I offered in Chapters 1 and 2. By thinking carefully about your topic, breaking your paper up into chunks, and writing a little at a time instead of a lot very quickly, you'll have time to put everything in this chapter into practice.

References

Ferro, Shane. 2015. "This One Piece of Viral Workplace Advice for Women Is Actually a Terrible Idea." *Business Insider*, July 9. Accessed July 11, 2015 from http://www.businessinsider.com/workplace-advice-for-women-not-to-use-the-word-just-is-terrible-2015-7.

Giles, Howard, Coupland, Justine, and Coupland, Nikolas. 1991. "Accommodation Theory: Communication, Context, and Consequence." In *Contexts of Accommodation*, edited by H. Giles, J. Coupland, and N. Coupland, 1–68. New York: Cambridge University Press.

Griffin, Cindy. 2011. *Invitation to Public Speaking*. Boston, MA: Wadsworth.

Holmes, Janet. 1990. "Hedges and Boosters in Women's and Men's Speech." *Language and Communication*, 10: 185–205.

Johnson, Rebecca. 2012. Twitter post (@johnsonr), October 18, 12:26 p.m., https://twitter.com/johnsonr/status/259012668298506240.

Nunn, Gary. 2015. "Is It Time We Agreed on a Gender-Neutral Singular Pronoun?" *The Guardian*, January 30. Accessed June 1, 2015 from http://www.theguardian.com/media/mind-your-language/2015/jan/30/is-it-time-we-agreed-on-a-gender-neutral-singular-pronoun.

Petrow, Steven. 2014. "Gender Neutral Pronouns: When 'They' Doesn't Identify as Male or Female." *The Washington Post*, October 27. Accessed June 1, 2015 from https://www.washingtonpost.com/lifestyle/style/gender-neutral-pronouns-when-they-doesnt-identify-as-either-male-or-female/2014/10/27/41965f5e-5ac0-11e4-b812-38518ae74c67_story.html.

Purdue Owl. 2015. "On Paragraphs." Last modified July 7, 2015. Accessed November 11, 2016 from https://owl.english.purdue.edu/owl/resource/606/01/.

5

Writing the Literature Review: Arguing for Audiences

Chapter Learning Outcomes

- Identify the common audiences for a literature review
- Answer the "So what?" question for readers
- Create effective arguments for a literature review
- Organize the literature review to enhance arguments

Chapter Features

- "Write Away"
- Student Spotlight
- Building Blocks

In the first four chapters, we've addressed a lot about the mechanics of writing, including concepts you can apply to any type of paper you might write for your class. Throughout the first four chapters, I've stressed how important it is to consider not only what you want to write about, but what your audience might

Composing Research, Communicating Results: Writing the Communication Research Paper,
First Edition. Kurt Lindemann.
© 2018 John Wiley & Sons, Inc. Published 2018 by John Wiley & Sons, Inc.

be interested in as well. This *connection* between you and the readers is an important one, as it helps you think about things from their point of view. This shift in perspective can aid you in everything from brainstorming topics to making arguments, making the writing process more of a *collaboration* between you and an imagined reader than simply a solitary activity. This shift helps you think about writing as being part of a *community* of scholars, including the readers of your paper and the people you cite in your paper. I'd like you to keep these themes of connection, collaboration, and community in mind as you read the rest of this book.

In the next few chapters, we're going to cover some common paper assignments you might encounter in almost any social science class. The first type of paper discussed in this chapter is a common assignment in many social science-related courses at both the undergraduate and graduate level: the literature review. At its most basic, this paper requires you to survey recent scholarly literature (and perhaps some popular literature like magazines and newspapers) related to a specific topic. Some instructors may ask you to pose hypotheses or research questions near the end of this paper, and others may ask you propose a specific study related to your review of the literature.

In any case, the term "literature review" is a bit of a misnomer. This paper should be more than simply a *review* of literature; it should make an argument. Note the subtitle of this chapter: Arguing for Audiences. Unfortunately, a lot of students follow a pattern of "This is a good topic, here's what this person found out about it, here's what some other people said about it, and in conclusion, here's what a bunch people concluded about this very important topic." As we'll see in later chapters, original data-driven research papers don't format literature reviews like this; those authors understand that they must make a case for studying particular topics in a certain way. A literature review, albeit one without a study following it, should be no different. When writing the literature review, you need to consider your readers just as you would with any paper: who your readers are, what they already know and what they need to know, and what format might be easier for them to understand.

Who Are You Writing For?

One of the biggest issues I see students struggling with in their papers is the concept of audience. Simply, students don't often consider for whom they are writing. As we discussed in previous chapters, this is understandable. Sometimes it's hard enough to find a topic that interests them. Then, there's so much research, often at a rushed pace because of the workload from other classes. Getting the citation style correct is also time-consuming. Given all this, it's sometimes difficult to take a step back and think about seemingly superfluous things like audience. As a result, students sometimes write "as noted in our class textbook..." If you are writing for a general academic audience, how are readers going to know what that textbook is? This question and others can be answered by more mindfully considering the audiences for literature reviews. Below, I cover some of the types of audience to consider when writing a literature review and how thinking about audience impacts what we might include in the review.

Academic audiences

Sometimes an instructor may not specify for whom you're writing. In an upper-division class, your instructor may assume you've already written several papers and have a good idea of the writer–reader relationship, which, as we've seen in the previous chapters, can inform every aspect of your paper, from brainstorming topics to the tone of voice in which you're writing. However, many students write numerous papers before they graduate, with barely a thought as to who their readers are. Or they assume the only reader for their paper is their instructor (Lindemann 2015). If you're writing your paper for an upper-division class, especially if it's for a communication class, your audience of readers will most likely be an "academic audience." Let's consider for a moment what this means.

An academic audience is made up of more than a *community* of academics, which obviously includes professors and published researchers. An academic audience also includes your classmates and other students in your major who may not be in your class. It's also beneficial to consider other college students not in your major as part of this academic audience. Interdisciplinary research is becoming a hallmark of many universities in the United States and has always been a tenet of European institutions (Flaherty 2015), so your imagined academic audience should be broader than just the students and teachers in your major. Regardless, the easiest and most common audience for a literature review, especially if you end up presenting a version of it at your school's research symposium or a regional or national conference, is an academic audience. However, they're not the only kind of readers you should imagine for your review.

General readers

Unlike academic audiences, many of whom are people you actually know (your instructor, your classmates, and other people at school), general readers are usually an imagined audience of readers who exist outside of your classroom walls. Of course, these folks exist "out there"; go to any bookstore (the ones that still exist) or go onto Amazon.com's book reviews and you'll see people who actually *still like to read*. General readers should be considered readers who, while lacking knowledge specific to your major, are interested in more than just video games and the goings-on of "famous" celebrity families on television.

Imagining a general readership can be useful in some instances, though probably not for your typical class papers. General readers likely won't understand any of the terminology specific to most of the class papers you write, and they won't understand why your paper is formatted and organized the way it is. So, imagine a general readership for your paper *only* if you're writing something that might be disseminated to the general public. These sorts of projects might include some of the things we covered in Chapter 1, like mission statements and reports. It's certainly useful to think of what knowledge general readers might have; doing so will help you consider which terms, theories, and concepts you need to explain in detail in your paper. And some scholars, such as H. L. "Bud"

Goodall, Jr. (2008), think social scientists should be "translating" academic research and writing for a general audience anyway. Of course, check with your instructor, but at least *consider* how your academic writing might need to be adjusted for a general readership.

Taken-for-granted knowledge and new knowledge

The knowledge of your academic readers and general readers may overlap, but in many cases it diverges. Obviously, academic readers will likely be familiar with the format of literature reviews and what such a paper is supposed to cover, whereas many general readers will not. Table 5.1 lays out some differences between the two types of readers and whether they'll "get" what you're trying to do in a literature review.

Notice that most of the rows in the right-side column include a "yes, if..." or a "probably not, unless..." caveat. Clearly, a literature review as most students have come to know it is not something familiar to general readers. As such, an academic audience of readers is the most appropriate audience for a literature review. As you can see in the middle column of the table, however, even some of the knowledge academics take for granted might need to be explained, for example specific theories you're using in your paper. Additionally, since academic readers aren't always in your major, you will still have to explain the phenomenon you're exploring and relate it to a "real-world" issue. With this in mind, let's consider the taken-for-granted knowledge academic readers might already have, as well as the new knowledge you might be providing them.

An imagined academic audience doesn't need to be convinced of the worth of social science research, either in the credibility of journal articles nor in the value

Table 5.1 Differences between academic and general readers

Areas of your literature review	Will academic readers "get it"?	Will general readers "get it"?
Area of research	• If related to your major, yes • If related to a "real world" issue, yes	If related to a "real world" issue, **yes**
Purpose of paper	Yes	**Yes**, if clearly laid out
Thesis	Yes	**Yes**, if clearly laid out
Backing	Yes	If examples are specific to your major, **probably not** unless they are universal
Theories	Yes, but will still require some explanation	**Probably not**, explain in layperson terms
In-text citation styles (APA, MLA, Chicago)	Yes, won't seem intrusive	**No**, it will probably seem weird
References or Works Cited page	Yes	**Maybe**, but not specific formatting choices

of conducting a literature review. These readers – who, remember, may include not just your classmates and instructors but, *hypothetically*, other like-minded students and people with an interest in your discipline – basically understand what you're doing in a review of literature. Granted, you're probably doing it because it's a class assignment, but these imagined readers won't question the utility of such an endeavor in a social scientific frame of thinking.

Write Away

On one side of a document or sheet of paper, list all the audiences you might have for your literature review, including the names of people you know personally if applicable (family, friends, etc.). On the other side, list what you think they know about your topic, theories, and so on.

   Then take another look at the list. If all these people are truly in the audience for your paper, be sure to explain things thoroughly so these particular readers will understand. Check off each name or group of people once you think you've addressed in your review what they know and don't know.

It's also important that you don't assume these readers are familiar with your class setting, environment, and specific research conditions. For example, referencing your school's database or library in your literature review is not taken-for-granted knowledge on the part of your readers. A student at San Diego State University (where I teach) should not write "I searched keywords on San Diego State University's Love Library's Communication and Mass Media Complete Database." An imagined audience of academic readers will wonder "What is this?" You may think including such information enhances your credibility, showing that you've actually done some research on academic databases and didn't just Google terms. But because it's very specific to your personal experience, including such information will only be distracting, and won't enhance your argument.

   This is true when referencing specific research conditions and settings as well, unless they are explained properly. You may be doing original, data-driven research, disseminating surveys to people, interviewing others, or maybe even observing them. A literature review will also be a part of these studies. However, you don't want to reference specific sites and settings with no context for readers. Take, for example, an actual qualitative research project conducted by two students, addressed in the first Student Spotlight of this chapter.

Student Spotlight: What's Taken-For-Granted Knowledge?

Two students in an undergraduate ethnography and communication class wanted to study the communication of community in "slacklining." Slacklining is a phenomenon popular in Southern California. Slackliners connect nylon bands of varying lengths between two or more trees and walk them like a tightrope, sometimes doing flips and jumps. The student authors quoted below interviewed and observed these slackliners for a semester.

In their introduction to their literature review, they wrote, "During the early phases of research, Author Two encountered a freshman student on campus slacklining in front of Viejas Arena." Viejas Arena is a popular concert and sports venue on campus at San Diego State University. This is the first time they have introduced readers to their research setting.

Will academic general readers know this arena, where and what it is? Probably not. This is not taken-for-granted knowledge. These authors needed to contextualize this information before launching into a review of the relevant literature. Consider what types of information in your own literature review might be too specific for general academic audiences. This might include locations and people known primarily in your immediate community.

By the end of this section, you should have thought about the *community of readers* for whom you're writing. You should also have thought about the differences between taken-for-granted and new knowledge in making a *connection* with these readers. As if this wasn't complicated enough, I'm going to add another layer to your audience: the scholars whose research you're going to cite in your review of literature. Thinking about entering into a conversation with a community of scholars is another important part of considering an audience of readers.

Engaging a community of scholars

Considering taken-for-granted and new knowledge on the part of the readers requires you to imagine yourself in dialogue with a *community of scholars*. These scholars are the people whose work you cite, the writers whose articles you read to get ideas, and the thinkers whose work you're going to build upon in the literature review. Author and scholar Sarah J. Tracy (2013) asks us to imagine a "conceptual cocktail party" to which you invite scholars. In other words, think about all the people you've come across in your reading. Imagine a party in which the main topic of discussion is the topic for your literature review (that's a rager, for sure!). Now ask yourself: Whom do you want to invite? Which people might have interesting things to say to each other? Why? When you've answered these questions, you've got a good idea of the community of scholars with whom you're conversing.

Just like successfully hosting a party, writing a literature review is about making introductions, making connections, and keeping guests engaged. This community of scholars will need introductions to each other. If you're the host of the party, you don't want to be rude. You should introduce them to each other and tell them what they have in common with each other.

Building Blocks

To get your "party guests" (the people you cite in your literature review) talking to each other, try making a list with following columns:

1) COLUMN 1: The guest's name and main published work you're citing in your literature review.

2) COLUMN 2: The guest's areas of interest you're drawing on in your literature review (this could be topics, theories, and opinions on a particular issue).

3) COLUMN 3: The other party guests you think that author has a lot in common with.

If you haven't guessed yet, each row *across* your page can now be thought of as a paragraph in your literature review. Of course, you'll need a topic sentence for that paragraph, as we've discussed in the previous chapter. So:

4) COLUMN 4: A possible topic sentence you think encapsulates the viewpoints and topics of each row across your page.

As long as you make sure your topic sentences serve as adequate backing statements or reasons for your claim, you essentially have the content for each paragraph in your literature review.

Your readers should be engaged as well, so you'll need to point out how what these scholars have to say is of interest to your readers. And as if all this weren't enough to think about, you'll also have to try and keep everyone talking about the same thing: your topic!

This isn't as hard as it seems, though. You just have to remember what we covered in Chapter 4 about topic sentences and the TESLA Method. Let's apply that method to engaging a community of scholars in a literature review:

1) Start with a **T**opic sentence (this is your welcome to the guests attending your party and telling them why you invited them).
2) **E**xplain and evaluate past research (this is your introduction of one scholar to another, telling each what they have in common).
3) **S**upport your own argument (this is you telling your guests what you have in common with them).
4) **L**ink back to topic sentence (this is your reminder to your guests as to why you invited them).
5) **A**nd – transition to the next paragraph, idea, point, or sub point (this is you moving the conversation along to a different, but related, topic).

Applying this method will help you avoid the all-too-common pattern found in many students' literature reviews I mentioned at the beginning of this chapter: devoting one paragraph to summarizing each study. Just as at a party you wouldn't want each guest in a corner of the room by themselves, not talking to anyone until you go up to each one and speak, you don't want the "guests" in your literature review relegated to one paragraph each. You want everyone in conversation with each other. Of course, people may not talk to each other (or read your paper) if they're not interested in the topic, so you also need to consider why people want – and need – to know about your topic.

Why Do Your Readers Need to Know This?

Academic audiences may not have questions about the value of a literature review or the sources you cite in it, but these readers will have questions about why your topic is important and why they should keep reading. Thinking about topic sentences using the TESLA method will help you keep them reading because, as we've already explored, your thesis should be composed of supporting statements, each of which can be your topic sentence. In short, the argument in your literature review should convince your readers that they need to know about your topic.

Thinking about the literature review as an argument requires us to consider why our readers need to know the information we're presenting to them. Many students, and even a lot of published scholars, fail to make the case for their research; they just assume, "Hey, you're reading a scholarly article, you must care about scholarship." What will help you make an argument for your readers, however, is to answer the "So what?" question. There are two main areas that you should address in answering this question: a practical need and a theoretical need.

Practical need: Applied understanding

Your first answer to the "So what?" question should be: because a comprehensive review of the literature surrounding your topic is useful, fulfills a practical need to make things better by offering readers enhanced skills and understanding, and/or sheds light on a problem in our society. For example, in a literature review about communication and aging, one undergraduate student answered the "So what?" question by noting that we face an aging population as health care gets better, which affects older and younger readers (the younger readers will presumably have to eventually take care of the older ones), and that an aging population also places a burden on our health-care industry (which could affect not only health-care workers but all of us who pay for insurance). She argues that,

> Communication can become a problem when they [the elderly] cannot keep up with these changes in their lives and the changes to society, which leads them to see the world differently than younger people. This creates an issue for their children and caregivers, who now need to change their forms of communication to be able to effectively communicate with parents or patients, or to achieve a level of understanding that avoids miscommunications or hurt feelings.

Clearly, this student's paragraph answers the "So what?" question. She attempts to appeal to a wide variety of academic audience members by illustrating a practical need, which her review goes on to address.

One can make an argument about almost any well-researched paper topic to respond to the "So what?" question. If you do a preliminary database search (see Chapter 2) with some keywords and find there's already some research out there, you can be assured there's enough relevancy in your topic to illustrate a practical need. However, if you find little to no research, it doesn't mean your topic has no relevancy; it just means you need to do a bit more work to make it relevant to audiences. We addressed this notion in Chapters 2 and 3, but as reminder: you may need to think about your topic in a slightly different way to make the argument for a practical need for a literature review. For example, you may think a paper on communication in dog parks is irrelevant to most readers. But as one undergraduate student wrote:

> Today, dogs are commonly considered part of the family; so much so that they are replacing children in many households, inferred from the statistics that show households with dogs outnumber those with children (El Nasser 2011). According to the American Pet Products Association's National Pet Owners Survey (2014), 56.7 million households in the United States own at least one dog.

This student went on to cite scholars who note the importance of communication in establishing community, thereby making the leap from the practical (there are more households with dogs than with children in the United States, so dog ownership potentially affects many people) to the theoretical (the notion of community is a scholarly and well-researched one). One thing you may have noticed from the student's argument about dog parks is that she cites non-scholarly, popular press sources from websites and newspapers. Of course, you'll have to check with your instructor to determine how many of these non-scholarly sources you're allowed to use in your own paper. But sometimes answering the "So what?" question requires you to use non-scholarly sources.

Focusing on the second need for your literature review may force you to rely primarily on scholarly sources. As I noted earlier in this book (Chapter 2), Kurt Lewin tells us there's nothing so practical as a good theory. Nonetheless, I have separated the discussion of practical and theoretical needs in order to help you better understand all aspects of writing a literature review. They are equally important, though, when crafting a well-written paper.

Theoretical need: "Filling in the gaps"

There is another aspect to answering the "So what?" question. In addition to fulfilling a practical need with your review of literature, you should also be thinking about adding to the body of scholarly research on a topic. Often, this requires you to make an argument about the current landscape of scholarship on your topic, namely that it could be enhanced or extended by thinking about your topic in a certain way (this is, in part, what you will argue for in your literature review). This doesn't mean that you're criticizing the way scholars have conceptualized and applied a concept; but one argument you might make is that your review of the literature can add something to the existing body of research.

Student Spotlight

Addressing the gaps in existing research can often be a powerful way to answer the "So what?" question for your literature review. Many students don't think of themselves as qualified enough to critique existing literature in this way. They often think, "I'm just a student and these people I'm citing are published. Do I even know enough yet to point out the gaps in existing literature?"

With enough research, yes, you should be able to make such arguments. It's important to note that you're not necessarily calling others' research bad, shoddy, or subpar by making this argument. Instead, addressing a theoretical need simply means you're pointing out something others may not have previously considered, as this student does when writing about the socialization of new members into organizations. He explains:

> Within the socialization literature there is an apparent bias towards examining more traditional organizations such as white-collar businesses, schools, and corporate settings (Kramer and Miller 2014). Despite this inherent bias in the literature towards more traditional organizations, it is important to also take the time to examine how socialization occurs in volunteer organizations. As volunteer organizations continue to thrive and grow all around our communities and the country, it is important to fully understand the scope of the literature regarding these institutions. This is because as these organizations grow, their power and influence will also likely grow, and they will continue to become a more integrated part of our daily lives.

You'll see that he doesn't criticize scholars for not focusing on volunteer organizations; he simply argues that this is a gap in the literature that needs addressing. True, he uses the word "bias," but in this context it doesn't mean discrimination or ignorance so much as a tendency. You'll also note that there is an argument for the practical need for a review of this literature embedded here. Volunteer organizations, he argues, are becoming pervasive throughout our society. As such, we need to examine their organizational processes more closely.

Ideally, the argument for your own review of literature will not address *either* the practical *or* theoretical needs, but will *combine* them when appropriate, as is the case in the above passage.

Organizing the Literature Review

A literature review, then, is not *just* a review of literature; it is an argument made with a particular set of readers in mind. And once your readers are addressed and your arguments solidified, you're faced with the task of organizing your review. Obviously, you should begin with an introduction and end with a conclusion, but what about in between? We're going to cover two ways you might think about organizing the content of your literature review.

Diamond shape: Specific to broad to specific

The first way you can think about your literature review is to see it as a diamond shape: narrow or specific at the beginning, wide or broad in the middle, and specific at the end (Figure 5.1).

Obviously, your introduction will be more specific than the body of your paper in the sense that you should use one incident from the news, a hypothetical

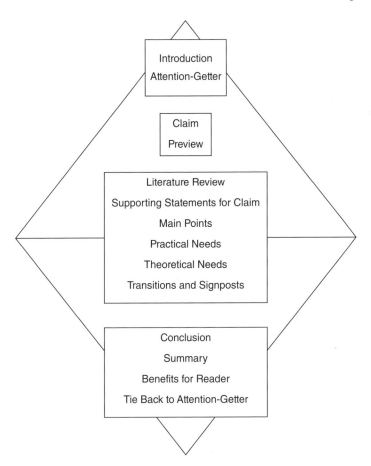

Figure 5.1 Diamond shape for literature reviews

situation, or some other narrowly focused concept to get your audience's attention. Once you move from the attention-getter, your introduction will likely get a bit broader as you introduce the concepts you'll be covering in the rest of paper, including a claim and a preview of the paper's main points.

Student Spotlight: Diamond-Shaped Organization

To better understand the diamond shape for a review of literature, let's take a look at the topic sentences and transition statements from an actual student paper. This particular student wrote about gender norms in a popular academic activity in the United States: collegiate debate. Rather than include the entire literature review here, I've included topic sentences. Consider each of the first few topic sentences in her literature review. Note how her scope moves from narrow to broader then back to a narrower area.

NARROW In the contemporary world of collegiate debate there are in-groups and out-groups. [*In this paragraph she introduces the notion of*

Communities of Practice, large groups of people who learn to cooperate and coalesce around the norms associated with a particular task or activity]

BROADER These Communities of Practice communicate norms and trends to competitors, coaches, and the community itself. [*Notice how the author moves from in- and out-groups to all people involved in the activity*]

BROADER I argue this type of feedback goes further than implying that women be more like men: it solidifies society's glass-ceiling stereotypes and, starting from a very young age, teaches women they are inferior to men. [*The literature review has broadened even more to address what is commonly called "the glass ceiling," an invisible barrier that exists for women in the workforce, enabling them to see where they might advance to but preventing them from doing so*]

BROADER In today's corporate world, a glass ceiling exists for women, particularly when they reach the upper levels of the corporate ladder. [*The literature review has moved from collegiate debate to the corporate world*]

BROADER This normalization of male behavior in society is not only in the workplace or home atmosphere, it permeates every section of Western society. [*Now the author is addressing gender norms in Western society*]

NARROWER While the intercollegiate debate community is very good at discussing political issues and pushing the line on performative debate, it has still been very hesitant to examine and challenge problems within the community itself. [*The literature review returns to a focus on the activity and the issues within it*]

The benefits of a diamond shape organization are that it allows you to introduce your topic first, then detail the numerous practical and theoretical implications of your topic. This helps you to continue to appeal to readers by arguing that your topic is worthy of attention.

Of course, each main point in the body of your paper should not only build on the argument you introduced earlier, using supporting or backing statements as the topic sentences for certain paragraphs, but the paragraphs should build on each other. Remember the party you invited these guests to? Well, this is point at which they're conversing with each other. If we could translate that into a shape, it might be the broadest part of the diamond, where the most connections and conversations between your citations are happening.

As you wind down your main points and move into your conclusion, you should be focusing on specific benefits your paper will offer: the ways it will fill in the theoretical gaps we covered earlier, the guidance it can offer practitioners outside the walls of your classroom (a concept we also covered earlier in this chapter), and some specific takeaways you want your readers to remember after they put down your paper (or the device on which they're reading it).

Finally, your conclusion should include a concise summary of your points. It may also hark back to your attention-getter, or it may present a new scenario, real or hypothetical, you want your audience to consider. In either case, this portion of your paper will likely be more focused and narrow than the main body of the paper. In this sense, we're at the bottom tip of the diamond.

Reverse triangle: Broad to specific

Another way you might think about your literature review is simply going from broad to specific, like an upside-down or reverse triangle (Figure 5.2).

While the parts may be the same as the diamond-shape approach, the conceptualization is different. You'll still have an introduction of course, preferably with an attention-getter and preview. But in this format you'll start more broadly, presenting the reader with a broad overview of the state of the scholarship regarding your topic. Perhaps you'll give the reader a feel for the scholarly landscape by delving into the history of research on your topic. Or maybe you'll offer an account of the research on this particular topic.

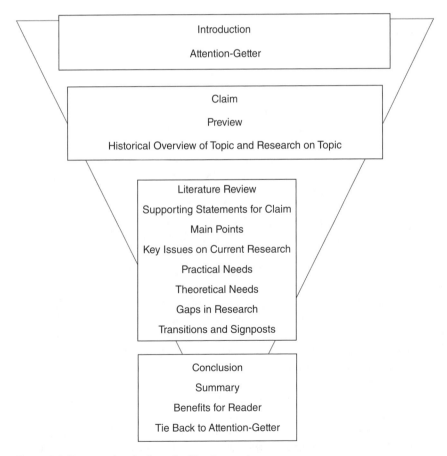

Figure 5.2 Reverse triangle shape for literature reviews

Student Spotlight: Reverse Triangle Organization

As with our previous style of organization, let's take a look at the topic sentences from an actual student paper to get a better grasp of the reverse triangle organization. These student authors conducted an original data-driven study of the acculturation practices of international students on U.S. university campuses. Acculturation is the process of people from another culture adapting to the host culture. Although the literature review only comprised about a third of their paper, it's still a good illustration of the reverse triangle style of organization. Consider each of the first few topic sentences and note how the scope moves from broad to narrow.

BROAD The prominence of international students on American university campuses and the increase in their population in the past few decades is not something to be ignored.

NARROWER International offices on U.S. campuses put a great effort in accommodating students to their new surroundings; however, these individuals will still go through acculturation. [*The authors move from discussing the increasing international student population in the United States to the process of adapting to U.S. culture*]

NARROWER There is much irony in the idea of universities welcoming international students into American culture when, in a lot of cases, international students spend the majority of their time in the host country with other international peers as opposed to "local" students from the host culture. [*The authors move from a broad discussion of acculturation to some specific critiques of the process; namely that international students may be more likely to socialize with other international students than with those from the host culture*]

NARROWER An important issue that should not be overlooked when studying international students and their transition to American culture is the well-being, both emotionally and physically, of these individuals. [*The literature review transitions to more specific consideration of the effects of acculturation*]

NARROWER If it isn't distressing enough for international students to adapt to a new educational and social environment, the adaptation to an entirely new culture can absolutely contribute to acculturative stress. [*The authors are now addressing aspects of international students' well-being, specifically stress*]

NARROWER When studying internationally, students are deprived of the social support and familiar means of communication that they would otherwise receive at home and that would allow them reassurance in stressful situations such as academic stress and second-language anxiety. [*The literature review narrows to a focus on types of stress and the lack of social support*]

In this reverse triangle organization, the authors first establish the worthiness of their topic by noting the large influx of international students on U.S. campuses. With this established as something academic audiences should care about, they are able to narrow their focus as the literature review progresses, first to acculturation, then to potential problems with this process, then to specific factors relating to one particular issue of acculturation: stress and social support.

In each subsequent section, you'll narrow the scope, focusing your examination of the literature on more specific issues, possibly gaps in the research or missing pieces of information. Each paragraph might focus on a missing piece of the puzzle, according to your argument. Or you might instead simply get more specific in your supporting statements, as in the famous syllogism commonly ascribed to the Greek philosopher Aristotle: *All men are mortal. Socrates is a man. Therefore, Socrates is mortal.* Although this example is most often used to demonstrate deductive reasoning and the use of a general statement (major premise), specific statement (minor premise), and conclusion, we can also view it as moving from general to specific. Indeed, deductive reasoning moves from general to specific as well. Note that the major premise broadly refers to "all men" (meaning *people*), and each subsequent statement gets more specific. The reverse triangle organization of a review of literature should follow a similar pattern.

Eventually, you'll end your literature review with the tip of the triangle, bringing your argument to a specific point and, as with the diamond-shaped format, offer readers a summary, a review, and several takeaways. You might also link back to your attention-getter here.

Citing Published Work: What Do I Say?

We've discussed in previous chapters when and how to cite published work. If you remember, I advised you in Chapter 3 to always try to paraphrase unless the language of the original article or story is poetic, vivid, and unique in a way that would be lost if you rephrased it. Whenever you directly quote a published piece, you should lead into that quotation or follow it up in your own words. For example, "Smith (2016) argues that ['direct quote' here] (p. 15)." Always remember to give the page number in whatever citation style you're using; the previous sentence is in APA style. Of course, you can also lead into a paraphrase of an author's work, or follow it up in your own words: "Smith (2016) contends that [insert a paraphrased summary here]." Notice that with APA style, no page number is needed for a paraphrased summary.

Since you'll be citing a lot of published work in your literature review, I want to revisit this concept of leading into and following up quotes and paraphrases, offering another helpful tip. We covered word choice and "flow" in Chapter 4. And if you remember, I suggested that you avoid repetitive wording. Well, the same goes for your lead-in and follow-up verbs. Are you always going to write that an author "argues"? What other verbs can you substitute? Contends? Stipulates? The possibilities are endless, but you should have a dozen or so "go to" words that you use. Table 5.2 offers some alternatives to the most commonly used phrases.

Table 5.2 Alternative lead-in and follow-up verbs

Commonly used lead-in and follow-up phrases	Possible alternatives
Argues	Contends, Posits, Offers
Writes	Summarizes, Stipulates, Asks [if posing a question], Concludes
According to…	As [the author] *use any of the terms above*

Chapter Summary

In this chapter we've covered who our audiences are, how to determine what they need to know about our topic, and how to convince them of our arguments in an organized way. Remember that academic audiences, the most appropriate audience for a literature review, already know some things. They understand the value of scholarly research, and they get the need for a particular citation style. However, while they are familiar with scholarly research and writing, they probably don't know the specifics of your theories and areas of research. Finally, the organization of a literature review, if done effectively, can enhance your argument. Whichever format you choose, you should avoid the one-study-per-paragraph pattern of organization. Remember that you're making an argument. You should use the scholarly and popular literature you find to support that argument in a way that makes sense to you and to the reader.

References

American Pet Products Association. 2014. "Pet Industry Market Size and Ownership Statistics." Accessed May 5, 2015 from http://www.americanpetproducts.org/press_industrytrends.asp.

El Nasser, Haya. 2011. "Fastest-Growing Urban Parks are for the Dogs." *USA Today*, December 8. Accessed May 6, 2015 from http://www.usatoday.com/news/nation/story/2011-12-07/dog-parks/51715340/1.

Flaherty, Colleen. 2015. "Cluster Hiring and Diversity." *Inside Higher Ed*, May 1. Accessed May 1, 2015 from https://www.insidehighered.com/news/2015/05/01/new-report-says-cluster-hiring-can-lead-increased-faculty-diversity.

Goodall, H. L. 2008. *Writing Qualitative Inquiry: Self, Stories, and Academic Life.* Walnut Creek, CA: Left Coast Press.

Kramer, Michael W., and Miller, Vernon D. 2014. "Socialization and Assimilation Theories, Processes, and Outcomes." In *The Sage Handbook of Organizational Communication*, edited by Linda L. Putman and Dennis K. Mumby, 525–547. Thousand Oaks, CA: Sage.

Lindemann, Kurt. 2015. "Dear Reader, (Do) You Know Who You Are: Voice and Audience in H. L. Goodall, Jr.'s Narrative Ethnography." *Qualitative Inquiry*, 22: 30–35. DOI: 10.1177/1077800409350060

Tracy, Sarah J. 2013. *Qualitative Research Methods: Collecting Evidence, Crafting Analysis, Communicating Impact.* Boston, MA: Wiley-Blackwell.

6

Application and Reaction Papers

Chapter Learning Outcomes

- Identify the purpose of application and reaction papers
- Identify the audience for application and reaction papers
- Create effective arguments for application and reaction papers
- Use scholarly literature as evidence and support for arguments

Chapter Features

- "Write Away"

Scholars don't invent theories and models simply for fun. They have an idea of how something works and apply it to "real-life" situations, data, and artifacts. In the same vein, your instructors may ask you to take one of these theories or concepts and use it to analyze something: a scholarly or popular press article, a book, a film, a speech. Scholars apply theories and models in their research to better understand various phenomena (Tracy 2013). Your instructors may ask you to apply a theory or model for this purpose as well. Or if they don't ask you to research a phenomenon on your own, then they might want to assess your knowledge of a theory or concept as a way of practicing and improving your analytical writing skills.

Composing Research, Communicating Results: Writing the Communication Research Paper,
First Edition. Kurt Lindemann.
© 2018 John Wiley & Sons, Inc. Published 2018 by John Wiley & Sons, Inc.

Similarly, you may be asked to write a reaction paper, in which you "react" or respond critically to an artifact like a newspaper column, a magazine or website story, or perhaps even an advertisement. A reaction paper is typically shorter than an application paper, and might even be something you write for a discussion board post for an online assignment via your course's Learning Management System (LMS). Some commonly used LMS platforms include BlackBoard, Moodle, Edmodo, and Desire2Learn. Regardless of their medium or length (in pages or words), reaction papers still require critical thinking and making a well-supported argument. In either case, applying concepts and theories, and making arguments about particular texts is a valuable skill. While the guidelines and tips for writing in the previous chapters of this book hold true for this type of paper, it's important to consider the ways you might apply those lessons to an assignment such as this.

Purpose

On one level, the purpose of a paper like this may be to apply a theory or concept to better understand an artifact. For example, a communication student might apply an interpersonal communication theory like Knapp's Staircase (1984) to a romantic comedy film, examining the way one or more relationships in the movie progress and dissolve. Knapp's model traces the stages of intimacy in a relationship and the interpersonal communication that often accompanies each stage. In applying this model to the relationships in a film, your instructor intends you to gain a better understanding of the ins and outs of the theory. This is usually the purpose behind this assignment, although in the application of a theory, model, or concept, you should also come to better understand that artifact, whether it's a book, a film, or some other text.

As always, check with your instructor and your class syllabus for the course and assignment learning objectives. It's possible there may be other intended purposes for such an assignment. Regardless of other learning objectives, however, there's another important purpose of such an assignment. It's learning the difference between *illustrating* a theory and *applying* a theory to gain further insight, both into the theory and into the artifact to which it's being applied. An illustration of a theory simply says to readers, "Here's this theory, and it can be applied to this artifact." An application of a theory says to readers, "Here's this theory, and by viewing this artifact through the lens of this theory we can gain additional insight into both the artifact and the theory." Both an illustration and an application can help you develop critical thinking skills. But the difference is that an application offers a more complex argument for readers.

Audience

The *community of readers* for a reaction or an application and analysis paper is likely an academic audience. General readers probably aren't interested in the intricacies of an academic theory and how it illuminates a given artifact. Certainly, there may be exceptions. The columnist Emily Nussbaum (2013) provided an interesting analysis in the *New York Times* of the television show *Mad Men* by loosely applying Freudian theory, writing that "'Mad Men' is brocaded with ultra-Freudian imagery – a gold violin, a rotten tooth – and it uses its camera less as a pair of eyes than as a proscenium, framing images as if they were posters" (para. 3). For newspaper readers, writers who examine popular culture must be fairly broad and avoid too much scholarly language. Nussbaum's language, while poetic, isn't scholarly. Your analysis for this paper will likely be more academic.

Remember that, unlike general readers, academic audiences won't usually be distracted by the inclusion of scholarly sources and language or citation styles. However, you'll still have to explain the concepts and theories you use to your audience. And you'll likely have to provide a detailed description of the artifact, as not all of your audience members may be familiar with it. Finally, you may need to do a little extra "thinking work" for the end of the paper to *connect* with your readers and make sure you provide them with some takeaways. With an analytical assignment like this one, it's easy to assume you've done all you need to by simply analyzing the artifact, but that attitude doesn't lead to the best possible conclusion for such a paper. We'll go over the important aspects of application and reaction papers below, but let's start with two concepts foundational to this type of writing: thinking critically and thinking argumentatively.

Thinking Critically

When they hear the word "critical," as in "critical writing" or "critical analysis," many students think of criticizing something. On the contrary, thinking critically doesn't necessarily mean criticizing something. The National Council for Excellence in Critical Thinking defines critical thinking as "actively and skillfully conceptualizing, applying, analyzing, synthesizing, and/or evaluating information gathered from, or generated by, observation, experience, reflection, reasoning, or communication, as a guide to belief and action" (Foundation for Critical Thinking 2013, para. 3). In short, thinking critically means taking something apart, determining how each part works, then putting the parts together again with a new perspective on the whole.

Think of your mind as a microscope, and your critical thinking facilities as a lens on that microscope (Figure 6.1). When you have your particular critical lens inserted, certain aspects of your artifact or text come into focus, and you may examine these aspects from a micro-, extremely close-up level. You can examine each aspect of the artifact or text in this way. Then, as you slowly decrease the magnification, you begin to see how each part is connected to the whole.

You can think of critical thinking in other ways using different senses, like sound, touch, and taste. You can think of it as listening to a piece of music, isolating the sound of each instrument separately, and then listening to the piece as a whole to really hear how everything works together. Or you could touch a sculpture or a motor, feeling each part, each curve, bolt, and edge, and consider how each connects to form the whole. Similarly, you may be able to isolate the tastes of particular ingredients from a dish you or someone else cooked. Ultimately,

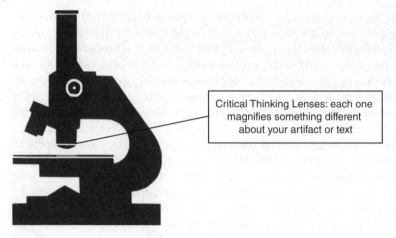

Critical Thinking Lenses: each one magnifies something different about your artifact or text

Figure 6.1 Microscope and critical thinking lens

taking things apart, or at least thinking about them separately, and then putting everything back together is a necessary part of critical thinking and the kind of analysis your instructor likely wants you to do with your papers.

With this definition in mind, critical thinking can encompass any number of activities. A car mechanic, when faced with an engine that isn't working properly, must apply critical thinking. She may already know how each part works, and based on the issues, might narrow the problem down to specific parts. However, she still has to disassemble all or some of the engine and examine each part to determine which one needs to be replaced. Likewise, we may consider an artifact – a speech, a film, a song – to be *problematic* in the sense that it potentially complicates our thinking about something. For example, back in the early 1980s a prevailing thought in the United States was that life was taking an unprecedented upturn as Americans became more prosperous. Rap group Grandmaster Flash and the Furious Five released their song "The Message" in 1982, with lyrics that provided a different take:

> My son said: Daddy, I don't wanna go to school
> Cause the teacher's a jerk, he must think I'm a fool
> And all the kids smoke reefer, I think it'd be cheaper
> If I just got a job, learned to be a street sweeper
> I'd dance to the beat, shuffle my feet
> Wear a shirt and tie and run with the creeps
> Cause it's all about money, ain't a damn thing funny
> You got to have a con in this land of milk and honey.
> *(Fletcher, Mel and Robinson 2005)*

Like of some of the best rap lyrics, this song, hailed by *Rolling Stone* magazine in 2012 as the best hip-hop song of all time, deconstructs (takes apart) what's commonly referred to as "the American Dream" by framing the business world ("shirt and tie and run with the creeps") as being as dishonest as any other activity inner-city African American men might engage in, questioning the very notion of the "American Dream" ("you got to have a con in this land of milk and honey"). Consistent with our definition of critical thinking, this song deconstructs our popular perception of an idea, then reassembles it into something with a new meaning. While not a rap song (although your instructor might allow you to analyze one), your paper should do something similar in the sense that it should *deconstruct* or take apart something to create new meaning for readers.

Write Away: Analyze Song Lyrics

Pick a song and look closely at the lyrics. You can Google the song name and "lyrics" and find any number of sites providing a transcription. But be sure to listen to it yourself to ensure the site's accuracy in reproducing the lyrics.

Next, provide a translation of each verse into a descriptive or explanatory sentence. At the end, write a one-sentence "lesson" a listener might take away from the song.

Doing this will get you ready for a description of the artifact for your analysis or application paper, and help you get into a "break it down" mindset to better offer your readers some takeaways.

The purpose of a reaction paper might also be to take apart something to create new meaning for readers. However, unlike an application and analysis paper, a reaction paper may be shorter and not require such an in-depth analysis. For example, after golfer Tiger Woods was caught cheating on his wife and his affairs were made public, Nike released an advertisement with a picture of Woods and the phrase "Winning takes care of everything" (ESPN.com News Services 2013). A reaction paper assignment about this ad might require you to identify the salient aspects of the ad, describe how the text and pictures interact with audiences' knowledge of Woods' personal problems, and articulate the values this advertisement espouses. You may provide anywhere from one to three paragraphs for each of these requirements. Nonetheless, you'd still be expected to write in complete sentences, using a thesis sentence, topic sentences, and transitions as discussed in Chapters 3 and 4. Of course, you may also be applying a theory, such as semiotics (Merrigan and Huston 2015), to your reading of this ad. For more on writing reaction papers, specifically pre-writing and organization, see the Further Reading section at the end of this chapter.

Thinking Argumentatively

So, we've got an idea of what it means to think critically. What does it mean to think argumentatively? Actually, you already know this. We've covered it in previous chapters. Thinking argumentatively means that, in whatever you're writing, including application and reaction papers, you clearly state a thesis and provide adequate backing for your thesis. Remember the Toulmin Method we discussed in Chapter 3, which includes using a claim and backing or support (the warrant is usually unstated). Also remember that a common fallacy about class papers is that they should be *either* opinion *or* argument. Of course, the correct way to approach any such paper is to understand that it is both. So, thinking argumentatively means supporting your opinion with backing in the form of concrete detail, descriptions, and relevant sources. All of this is what it means to think argumentatively.

Providing support

It's pretty clear, then, that a big part of thinking argumentatively means providing support for your claim. Unlike what you do in a literature review, though, providing support in application and reaction papers requires some concrete description you usually can't get from sources other than the artifact you're examining. Support for application and reaction papers should include detailed descriptions of the artifact itself. Remember, you're arguing that certain elements of the film, advertisement, and so on can be read a certain way by applying a critical lens. So, how do you accomplish the goal of providing specific concrete details? One way is to follow the SCEDU system: Scan, Choose, Examine, Describe, and Unpack:

The SCEDU Method of providing support

When writing an analysis or reaction paper, much of the support you offer will come in the form of concrete examples taken directly from your artifact. Use this method to generate these examples and work them into your analysis as support.

1) **S**can the artifact completely. If analyzing a film, watch it all the way through; if reacting to a news story, advertisement, cartoon, etc., read it through several times.
2) **C**hoose the most salient aspects. What are the film's pivotal scenes? What is the thesis of the story? What support is offered? What is foregrounded in the advertisement? Backgrounded?
3) **E**xamine each of the chosen aspects carefully. Pay attention to the composition, how each aspect works and why.
4) **D**escribe these aspects in complete sentences. Remember, the concrete examples you provide in your actual paper will come from your descriptive writing.
5) **U**npack your examples. Explain in complete sentences how these aspects function, and how they work together successfully and/or unsuccessfully as a whole.

First, *scan* your artifact. If you're examining a film, watch it all the way through. If you're reacting to a newspaper or magazine story, read it completely. If you're analyzing an advertisement, take some time to notice every aspect of it – the word placement, the images and their position on the page, the background and foreground, the colors, and so on.

Next, *choose* what you believe to be the most salient aspects of your artifact – a sentence or passage, an image, a scene. These are aspects that you believe represent the purpose, point, or argument of the piece. If responding to a film, be sure you're not retelling the story. Of course, perhaps a brief summary is necessary, but sometimes in retelling the story of a film to a friend we might gloss over thematic aspects and focus only on plot points or action. See Further Reading for some additional resources containing tips and guidelines for writing reaction papers.

After you've chosen these aspects, *examine* them using the scanning techniques you employed earlier. Focus on these details and note everything about them, writing down everything in a stream-of-consciousness fashion.

Using these notes, *describe* those aspects in complete sentences. Remember, these sentences may work their way into your actual paper, so to decrease the work you have to do on your paper, and to enable you to cut and paste when the time comes, put work into capturing as much concrete detail as possible.

Then, *unpack* these aspects by attempting to explain in writing: (a) how they function and (b) how they work in relation to the whole. "Unpacking" is similar to a word I used previously in this chapter: deconstructing. In each case, you're explaining, piece by piece, how this particular aspect works.

For example, let's say you're applying Marxist theory to the 2009 James Cameron movie, *Avatar*. Marxism, often confused with Communism but not the same thing, posits that one can better understand society by examining its socio-economic aspects and the political struggles of economic class and status (Elster 1986). After some review, you might think it an appropriate lens through which to examine the film. You might (spoiler alert!) choose a scene in which the military officials are talking about mining the planet Pandora for Unobtanium, a valuable mineral. The inhabitants of Pandora, the Na'vi, are peaceful and nature-loving, something in direct contrast to the military perspective on which you're focusing. In providing support for your thesis, which might be something like "*Avatar* offers a critique of the military-industrial complex by juxtaposing two perspectives on the role of the environment in human progress," you could describe the appearance of the military officers, describe the interior of their headquarters and contrast it with the Na'vi village, and compare the way each group of people talks about their relationship to the environment.

Now, you may have excellent support for your analysis in the form of detailed descriptions from your artifact, generated by following the method outlined above. Unfortunately, for a class paper this usually isn't enough. Many instructors will want you to integrate your analysis with what others have said. Therefore, it's important we consider how you might link your analysis to relevant scholarly literature.

Linking to scholarly literature

Just because you're offering support for your analysis or reaction in the form of concrete detail, you shouldn't neglect to cite scholarly literature as well. As always, check with your syllabus, assignment descriptions, grading rubrics, and instructor to see whether this is required and, if so, how many sources you're required to cite. But ultimately, you shouldn't be citing sources because you're required to; you should be citing sources because doing so helps readers better understand your analysis by contextualizing it in the landscape of scholarship surrounding your topic and/or artifact.

And just as with literature reviews (see Chapter 5), follow Sarah J. Tracy's (2013) metaphor for linking to scholarly literature: the conceptual cocktail party. Invite guests you think would be interested in discussing your topic, and make sure they get to the party early; in other words, cite some of them in your second or third paragraph. Continue talking to your guests throughout the party (be sure to cite them throughout your paper where appropriate). And, finally, say goodbye to your guests by citing at least some – maybe the guests of honor, or those most important to your paper – in your conclusion.

With a literature review it may be fairly obvious how to link your own thoughts and ideas to relevant scholarly literature. With an application or reaction paper, however, it may be less clear. So, let's go back to our example of the film *Avatar*. After you've watched the film once, then scanned, chosen, examined, described, and unpacked relevant examples, you'll need to contextualize your analysis in the larger scholarly dialogue: about science fiction as a genre and/or about the film itself. Although other writers won't make your arguments for you, linking to the scholarly literature is a way to *connect* with a scholarly *community* and *collaborate* with them in your analysis.

You might tell readers what other critics have concluded about the film, or perhaps how scholars have analyzed the utility of science fiction as a genre to comment on human relations and humans' relationships to the environment. Of course, you would correctly cite sources as per the citation style required, taking care to paraphrase and not simply quote directly, which will ensure that you're fully integrating others' viewpoints into your own argument. After doing this, you might put it all together to explain to your readers what this means. This might happen in the last few paragraphs of the body of your paper, or in the conclusions.

It seems, then, that we might be missing one step from our method of generating support for an analysis or reaction paper. So, let's add another to the SCEDU method discussed earlier. Finally, *link* to scholarly literature by telling readers: (a) what other scholars have said about your artifact generally (the focus of your artifact), or specifically (the artifact itself); (b) how what you've said provides additional insight into what these scholars have concluded: Does your analysis support theirs, contradict theirs, and/or offer a new way of understanding what they've said? This extension prompts a revision in the method, reflected in the list below:

The SCEDUL Method of providing support
When writing an analysis or reaction paper, much of the support you offer will come in the form of concrete examples taken directly from your artifact. Use this method to generate these examples and work them into your analysis as support.

1) **S**can the artifact completely. If analyzing a film, watch it all the way through; if reacting to a news story, advertisement, cartoon, etc., read it through several times.
2) **C**hoose the most salient aspects. What are the film's pivotal scenes? What is the thesis of the story? What support is offered? What is foregrounded in the advertisement? Backgrounded?
3) **E**xamine each of the chosen aspects carefully. Pay attention to the composition, how each aspect works and why.

4) **Describe these aspects** in complete sentences. Remember, the concrete examples you provide in your actual paper will come from your descriptive writing.
5) **Unpack your examples.** Explain in complete sentences how these aspects function, and how they work together successfully and/or unsuccessfully as a whole.
6) **Link to scholarly literature.** How does your analysis match up with other scholars' analysis? Does yours support, contradict, or extend theirs? In what ways?

Making conclusions

Part of explaining what it all means involves offering readers some takeaways. In other words, consider what you want your readers to remember after they've put down the paper. As you might guess, what you offer here will probably be a bit broader than the focused analysis you presented in the body of the paper. So, allow yourself to think bigger. In the above example of an analysis of the film *Avatar*, you might explain to readers how your analysis can be applied to other movies that depict environmental issues, the military, or intercultural relations. You might also explain to readers how the film, the highest-grossing worldwide film of all time (IMBD 2015), created new technologies of filmmaking that could be used in real-life applications outside of Hollywood. Finally, you might point to some other potential areas of analysis for *Avatar* (and perhaps other science-fiction films), for example, disability studies (the main character is disabled).

Remember that this is *your* argument. Don't feel intimidated by other writers who have published essays on this topic. A common mantra for student authors when reaching the conclusions section of any paper – a literature review, an analysis or reaction paper, or even a data-driven study – is to worry, "These people have all published on this topic. Who am I to say that my paper contradicts or extends their scholarship?" Well, at this point in writing the paper, you've done a careful reading (hopefully several) of your artifact. Guess what? You're an expert! Don't be shy about asserting your conclusions. Often, instructors want to see critical thinking in papers; even if they disagree with some of what you have to say, they appreciate original arguments. Drive those home in your conclusions.

Chapter Summary

In this chapter we've covered the common purposes and audiences for analysis and reaction papers, as well as some guidelines on thinking critically and making arguments. We've also discussed the SCEDUL method for generating support for arguments in the form of concrete details. By the time you finish such a paper, you should consider yourself an expert on your artifact. That should help alleviate any intimidation you might feel commenting on scholars' published works. Remember: instructors value critical thinking and original arguments. All arguments, based as they are on someone's opinion, can foster disagreement. As long as your arguments are well supported, instructors will appreciate them even if they disagree with them.

References

Cameron, James, dir. 2009. *Avatar*. Film. Los Angeles: 20th Century Fox. DVD, 2010.

Elster, Jon. 1986. *An Introduction to Karl Marx*. Cambridge, UK: Cambridge University Press.

ESPN.com News Services. 2013. "Nike's Tiger Woods Ad Draws Criticism." March 29. Accessed May 7, 2015 from http://espn.go.com/golf/story/_/id/9100497/ nike-winning-takes-care-everything-tiger-woods-ad-draws-critics.

Fletcher, Ed "Duke Bootee," Mel, Grandmaster Melle, and Robinson, Sylvia. 2005. *The Message*. In *The Message*. Dbk Works. B0007WFX9O CD.

Foundation for Critical Thinking. 2013. "Defining Critical Thinking." Accessed May 6, 2015 from http://www.criticalthinking.org/pages/defining-critical-thinking/766.

IMBD. 2015. "All Time Box Office: Worldwide." Accessed June 8, 2015 from http://www.imdb.com/boxoffice/alltimegross?region=world-wide.

Knapp, M. L. 1984. *Interpersonal Communication and Human Relationships*. Boston, MA: Allyn & Bacon.

Merrigan, Gerianne, and Huston, Carole L. 2015. *Communication Research Methods*. New York: Oxford University Press.

Nussbaum, Emily. 2013. "Faking It: *Mad Men*'s Don Draper Problem." *The New Yorker*, May 20. Accessed May 5, 2015 from https://www.google.co.uk/?gws_rd= ssl#q=%E2%80%9CFaking+It:+Mad+Men%E2%80%99s+Don+Draper+Problem.% E2%80%9D+.

Rolling Stone. 2012. "The 50 Greatest Hip-Hop Songs of All Time," *Rolling Stone*, December 5. Accessed May 6, 2015 from http://www.rollingstone.com/music/lists/ the-50-greatest-hip-hop-songs-of-all-time-20121205/grandmaster-flash-and-the- furious-five-the-message-19691231.

Tracy, Sarah J. 2013. *Qualitative Research Methods: Collecting Evidence, Crafting Analysis, Communicating Impact*. Boston, MA: Wiley-Blackwell.

Further Reading

See http://leo.stcloudstate.edu/acadwrite/reaction.html for some great tips on pre-writing and organization.

For more helpful tips on how to approach writing reaction papers, you can also check out http://public.wsu.edu/~moonlee/WritingReactionPaper.html.

Writing about a film can be difficult, so in addition to the suggestions in this chapter, check out http://academic.regis.edu/jroth/WRITING%20FILM% 20RESPONSE%20PAPERS.htm for more guidance.

7

Writing Empirical Research Papers

Chapter Learning Outcomes

- Identify the common parts of an empirical research paper
- Distinguish best practices for writing empirical research papers
- Make effective arguments in empirical research papers

Chapter Features

- Student Spotlight
- "Write Away"
- Engaging Ethics
- Building Blocks

So far, we've discussed two common types of papers you might be required to write in your classes: the literature review and the application and reaction paper. There's another type of paper you may be asked to write: the empirical research

Composing Research, Communicating Results: Writing the Communication Research Paper,
First Edition. Kurt Lindemann.
© 2018 John Wiley & Sons, Inc. Published 2018 by John Wiley & Sons, Inc.

paper. Many advanced courses at the undergraduate and graduate levels require some sort of original, data-driven paper, especially if they are courses designed to teach you a particular research method. This is *not* a how-to chapter on conducting research studies, quantitative or qualitative. There are plenty of great books out there to help you with that (see Further Reading at the end of this chapter). What this chapter is designed to help you with, however, is the *writing* of those studies. There are certainly best practices for writing *any* type of paper, on which Chapters 1–4 focused. But this chapter will focus attention more on writing a data-driven research paper.

Empirical papers are different from literature reviews and application/reaction papers in several important ways. To distinguish between these types of papers, let's clarify what "empirical" means in the context of social science research. *Empirical research* simply refers to research that involves, and is verifiable by, observation, as opposed to research based on theory or logic. While some folks believe empirical research refers only to quantitative or statistical research, perhaps because of the term "verifiable" (commonly meaning "proven true" by statistical measurements), empirical research can also be qualitative, involving observations and interviews. There are, however, some differences in the way you might write a study depending on its methodological approach, most of which have to do with conventions of writing associated with each approach (again, see Further Reading at the end of this chapter for more on planning and executing different research designs).

While there are important differences between papers written with different methodological approaches, there are just as many similarities. With this in mind, we'll first cover the crucial parts of an empirical research paper common across any type of methodological approach. We'll end this chapter with a closer examination of these differences and then focus on the types of empirical research paper common in most social science classes.

Introduction, Justification, and Rationale

Regardless of how you gathered and analyzed your data – through surveys, interviews, observations, or reflections on personal experience – there are some common parts of an empirical research paper. More advanced writers may vary the structure, something we'll discuss at the end of this chapter, but it's a safe bet that any such paper will have the same sections somewhere in it. The first important section of a research paper contains several parts: the introduction, justification, and rationale. Importantly, these aren't separate; rather, together they comprise the first section of your paper that typically comes before the literature review. While most would normally call this the introduction, it should do more than just introduce your topic.

Remember that while you may have been working on your paper for a long time, perhaps the entirety of your course – with intermittent feedback from your teacher and maybe even your classmates – the general academic reader won't have any idea of your topic before reading the first few lines (although your title will probably contain some hints). As such, you should let the reader know in the first paragraph what the focus of your paper is. This will be, of course, after an attention-grabbing lead-off sentence or two. Also remember that not only does your reader need to know what your paper is about in the first few paragraphs, but your reader also needs a *reason* to keep reading. This is why your introduction should not only introduce your topic but also provide a justification or rationale for the topic: Why is this topic important? Why does this study need to be conducted? Each of these areas is addressed in the Student Spotlight below.

Student Spotlight: Introduction, Justification, and Rationale

While teachers and even some classmates comprise a "captive audience of readers," meaning they basically *have* to read your paper, a general academic audience who can stop reading at any time needs a reason to *continue* reading. You can offer them this in the first few paragraphs. As we saw in Chapter 3, every paper is an argument, and an argument can be made about virtually any topic.

Consider the following, from an actual empirical research paper written by an undergraduate, and see if you can determine the topic from the first few sentences:

> The years that a young adult spends in college are notoriously known as a time for individuals to explore and discover themselves by developing their own morals, beliefs, and values. People form their faith in many different stages throughout life. However, the period between the ages of 18–25 tends to be when individuals are in the process of separating their identities from their worldviews (Fowler 1997). While a multitude of factors can affect this individual development, one of the most influential is religion. Religious affiliation can pervade every aspect of a young adult's life, and can be revealed, sustained, and promoted through communication.

Pretty obvious, isn't it? This student's paper is about religiosity and communication among university students. The reader doesn't have to go too far into the paper to get a sense of the focus of the paper and the general direction of her argument. While we may not yet be presented with her claim, we know that this author believes religion to be an important factor influencing communication among young adults.

The author goes on to provide a justification, or rationale, for her study in the next paragraph:

> In a society that practices freedom of religion, religiosity becomes a significant part of everyday life. In fact, the *U.S. Religious Landscape Survey* (Pew Forum 2008) studied 35,000 Americans and found that approximately 80% have some sort of religious affiliation, with the largest majority identifying as Christian. Therefore, as religious talk is very much a part of conversation in the U.S., it is important that college students learn how to communicate across religious and ethical differences in order to live cohesively (Kunzman 2012). Religion helps people develop their own worldview, which in turn affects the way they act, form relationships, and interact with those around them.

Although this author could have provided even more source citations to tell readers, "Hey, this is an important topic and you should pay attention," notice that she offers some relatively recent sources to support her argument that religiosity among university students is an important topic worth reading about. Even readers who don't consider themselves religious may find other reasons to keep reading: they might be college students, they might teach college students, or they might have family members who are or will be attending university. In short, the author does her best to cut across a wide range of reader interests in making her argument.

In these first two paragraphs of the author's paper, then, readers are told what the topic is, why it's important, and why they should continue reading. This Student Spotlight provides a good example of how to use the introduction to your paper as more than just an "introduction." I'll refer to this example throughout this chapter, expanding on how we might proceed given a particular methodological approach.

Revisiting the Literature Review

As we discussed in Chapter 5, the literature review isn't simply a "this scholar said this, this scholar said that" section of your paper that simply summarizes relevant literature. The literature review is your opportunity to make an argument. When it is part of an empirical research paper, the literature review should extend the rationale for your study offered in your introduction. Unlike in a literature review assignment, however, you may not be able to articulate your argument for an empirical research paper until you have gathered and analyzed your data. Nonetheless, the literature review is the best place to start writing an empirical research paper, even if you have to revise it after your study is done. There's a famous saying that "the map is not the territory." What this means is that a map is important, but it doesn't represent *everywhere* you may want to go. Translated to the art of writing a paper, this old saying means the following: your literature review can formulate the map for your paper – what you plan to focus on, the arguments you plan to make – but, depending on what your data tells you, you may need to explore other areas. So it's important to remember to be flexible when writing the literature review, keeping in mind that you will likely be revising your literature review after you've gathered and analyzed your data.

Quantitative approaches

For a quantitative approach, the literature review will usually end with research questions and/or hypotheses. The literature review should make an argument that logically leads the reader to these items. In essence, the literature review should give readers a sense of a logical conclusion, as in "therefore ... we can guess these things [hypotheses] and must ask these questions [research questions]." The best research questions are simple and straightforward, and will likely ask about the relationship between two variables. If we were to take our earlier Student Spotlight paper as an example, we might ask:

RQ$_1$: How does the degree of religiosity affect … [insert any number of communication concepts here: self-disclosure, conflict style, attachment style, etc.]?

Notice the subscript "1" after the "RQ"; this is appropriate if we are asking more than one research question. Otherwise, we would just put "RQ." While this research question focuses on the effect of one thing on another, we don't have to ask a question about the relationship between two variables or concepts. In the above example, we could just ask separate questions about each concept or variable, but those questions are sometimes too broad. For example, the question of what conflict styles are used among college students may be too wide-ranging to determine with one study, let alone a paper for which research has to be conducted during the course of one class.

If we were to ask the above research question, our literature review would necessarily have to include a discussion of not only religiosity, but also our second variable – self-disclosure, conflict style, or attachment style. Further, we would have to make the argument that a discussion will enable these two concepts to fit together in a logical way. In other words, we couldn't just say to our readers, "Let's put these two things together and study the effects." There has to be a *reason* we're discussing these two concepts, and we need to convince our readers of that reason. Obviously, the more variables or concepts about which we're asking questions, the more we need to include, and argue for, in our literature review.

If, based on our literature review, we believe we have enough information to make a *prediction* about the relationship between two variables, we might pose hypotheses. One hypothesis, based on a literature review stemming from the earlier Student Spotlight example, may look like this:

H$_1$: The higher the religiosity of college students, the lower their degree of self-disclosure with those perceived to be low in religiosity.

Remember, the subscript numeral 1 is only appropriate if we are posing more than one hypothesis; otherwise, we simply use "H." What we're predicting with this hypothesis is that if a college student measures high on a scale of religiosity, they may engage in less disclosure with students he or she perceives as being less religious. We may make this prediction based on a review of literature that explains that, while being openly religious on college campuses is more common today, there still exists a hesitancy among students to disclose their religious beliefs. We may also come to understand that we disclose personal information to others whom we perceive as similar to us, as most self-disclosure research has found. Putting these two bits of information together, we can lead our readers to the prediction posed by our hypothesis. As we'll see with posing qualitative research questions, language is important not only in the literature review, but also in the wording of our questions and hypotheses.

Qualitative approaches

In many ways, writing a literature review for an empirical study employing qualitative approaches is no different than writing a literature review for a quantitative study. The literature review should be thought of as an argument not only for the focus of your paper – a justification and rationale – but also one that provides readers with reasons for asking the research questions you pose. One major difference, however, is that a qualitative approach doesn't usually lead to posing hypotheses. The goal of empirical research conducted in what is alternatively referred to as the Discovery paradigm (Merrigan and Houston 2015), the Sociopsychological paradigm (Craig 1999), or more commonly the Post-Positivist paradigm, is usually to conduct measurements of variables to be able, eventually, to predict outcomes. The goal of what is usually referred to as the Interpretivist paradigm, in which most qualitative research is conducted, is to understand, but not necessarily predict, outcomes across a wide variety of contexts and populations. As such, empirical studies that employ qualitative methods won't commonly pose hypotheses. Instead, these studies will usually offer only research questions.

Taking the Student Spotlight paper as our ongoing example, let's say that, instead of a quantitative approach using surveys we're going to adopt a qualitative approach that involves interviewing college students. Instead of predicting a relationship between variables, we will pose research questions at the end of our literature review. And just as precise language is important in posing hypotheses, the use of language in writing qualitative research questions is equally important. For example, since we're not measuring relationships between variables, we will want to avoid language that implies measurement: words like "effect" (What is the effect of A on B?) and "affect" (How does A affect B?) imply a relationship between variables (A and B). As such, we usually want to avoid these words in a qualitative research question.

Instead, we want to ask questions that involve a "how" or a "why." For example, we might ask:

> RQ: How do self-identified "religious" college students disclose their beliefs to non-religious students?

Notice the absence of a subscript for this research question. While qualitative studies can ask more than one research question, they usually focus on fewer, more broad-ranging questions than quantitative studies. Also, notice that our research question in this instance is written to probe *how* something happens, in this case self-disclosure.

Write Away

Thinking about your topic, ask yourself: What do I want to know about this? Write a series of five questions, beginning each question differently. Use What, How, Why, When, and Who to start each question.

Next, ask yourself the following:

1) Is this question relevant to the class?
2) Does answering this question satisfy the paper assignment and its learning objectives (if there are any)?

3) Would I be able to answer this question given the time parameters? [*Depending on the length of your semester or quarter, and/or how long your instructor is allowing*]

4) Am I able to answer this question in a methodology I'm comfortable with? [*Asking about the relationships between variables implies measurement, which may require surveys, experiments, and quantitative analysis. Can you complete such a study?*]

5) What do readers need to know about my topic for this question to make sense? [*In other words, How can I logically lead them to this question?*]

Your answer to each of the questions above should provide a rough map of not only your study, but the areas you'll need to cover in your literature review. The questions should help you better understand which methodological approach you're invoking and adjust accordingly.

Methods: Argument and Explanation

So, you've made the argument for your readers, one that logically leads them to your hypotheses and/or research questions. Assuming you've already conducted your study, you must also explain to readers how you gathered and analyzed data. While this sounds simple, it's important to include a well-written methods section. Such a section ensures transparency on the part of the researcher; explaining to readers exactly what you did and how you did it allows readers to assess your credibility as a researcher and better understand your results or analysis section (more on that later).

Engaging Ethics: Getting Permission to Gather Data Using Human Subjects

It's important to check with your instructor about whether you are required to get permission from your school's Institutional Review Board (IRB) or Ethics Committee for the use of human subjects in research. Often, if research derived from data gathered from human subjects is intended to be presented outside the classroom or published, the researcher is required to get permission from her school's IRB. Sometimes, if the purpose of data-gathering is solely for teaching purposes, students may not have to go through the school's IRB. IRBs are in place to ensure the researcher does not cause harm (physical, psychological, or emotional stress, damage to a participant's reputation or good standing with the community, etc.) to participants.

For more information, see the appropriate webpage for your school's IRB. You may be required to go through a training program to receive certification. For more about the origins and importance of IRBs, see Tracy (2013).

Usually the second major section in an empirical research paper (following the literature review), the methods section is sometimes to most difficult for students to write. Ironically enough, this difficulty often stems from the fact that a methods section may have considerably fewer source citations than a literature review. This is because the methods section of a research paper is usually a straightforward, no-frills explanation of what you did and how you did it in terms of conceptualizing your study, gathering your data, and analyzing your data. A methods section will vary slightly depending on the approach, and I cover some of these differences below.

Writing the quantitative methods section

A methods section for a quantitative study must include several important descriptions. The first is a description of the participants, including demographic information relevant to the study, like age, race, marital status, etc. You should also explain how many participants were included in your study and how you determined who your participants would be – commonly called a sampling technique (Keyton 2014). Next, you should explain how you collected your data. Did you stand outside a building on a busy sidewalk and hand out surveys? Did you get an e-mail list from somewhere and send out an electronic survey? Did you stage a room to look like somewhere specific (a professor's office, for example) and invite people in under false pretenses? Be sure to explain any relevant details clearly and succinctly. Finally, what variables did you study? Describe them in layperson terms so readers understand not only the theoretical framing, taken from your literature review, but also how you used these terms in "real" research. This is called operationalization (Keyton 2014).

This methods section will often be written in the third person. As we discussed in Chapter 4, the third person should generally be avoided as it may prompt you to lapse into the passive voice. Nonetheless, the third person and even the passive voice are conventions of writing often used in quantitative studies, especially in the methods section. So, for example, a methods section for a quantitative study might read: "An initial random sample of 100 males and females ages 18–25 was garnered from classroom volunteer forms. The researchers then e-mailed the volunteers with additional questions and selected 50 participants based on those answers." Notice that the first sentence in this example is written in the passive voice; remember, if you can add "by zombies" to the end of the sentence and it is grammatically correct, you're writing in the passive voice. The second sentence in this example is obviously written in the third person; rather than using "we," the researchers call themselves "the researchers."

There is a method to the "madness" of writing in the passive voice and the third person voice for a methods section in a quantitative study, and that has to do with the paradigm in which the researchers are operating. Earlier we discussed that this paradigm may be called Sociopsychological or Post-Positivist. Since this paradigm emulates the hard sciences, let's consider a hypothetical example of a scientist mixing chemicals at a bench. It doesn't matter who is mixing the chemicals – age, race, gender, etc. – if they're doing "good" science, that's all that matters. It follows, then, that the methods section for an empirical research paper using quantitative methods won't use an "I"; just like the researcher mixing chemicals, the person *behind* the methods isn't important; the research should be considered on its own merits. Hence, the methods sections for a quantitative approach will go to great lengths to make sure the researcher is absent – no references to the researcher using "I."

Writing the qualitative methods section

A methods section for an empirical research paper using qualitative methods is similar to one detailing a quantitative approach: there should be clear, succinct, and easy-to-understand explanations of what the researcher did and how she did it. Additionally, qualitative research papers should describe the sites where observations were conducted, how interview participants were chosen, and how many hours and pages of transcription resulted from these procedures. Finally, as for a quantitative methods section, researchers here should describe how the data was analyzed.

Unlike in a quantitative methods section, however, these analytical procedures will not be statistical tests but descriptions of how the researcher came to understand, or *code*, her data. Such a description will often consist of how she literally went about collecting and understanding her data. Consider the detail in the following excerpt from an actual student paper. This student observed and interviewed people involved in a university's BDS movement, which is a group that promotes boycott, divestment, and sanctions against Israel until it recognizes Palestinian rights. He also analyzed this group's conflicts with the same campus's Jewish student group:

> Every other week, I attended Students for Justice in Palestine (SJP) and Students Supporting Israel (SSI) meetings. These two organizations are at the forefront of leading the pro- and anti-divestment communities. SJP leads the pro-BDS community and SSI leads the anti-BDS community. During these meetings, I would refrain from participating in group discussions in order to retain my unbiased approach to my study. Instead, I vigorously took field notes in order to obtain thick description. Simply observing both organizations in a public setting would not have given me any insight into the massive amount of preparation needed for these public verbal jousting sessions, otherwise called open forum debates. I not only took field notes of the discussions and interactions relating to the overall divestment movement, but also of the comradery and friendships developed by members of both organizations.

Note how clear and concise this student's description of data-gathering procedures is here. His fieldwork and observations are presented to the reader in a way that allows the reader to understand exactly how he approached his observations and when and where he conducted them. He also includes some descriptive language ("verbal jousting sessions") to give readers a sense of what the meetings were like, something he elaborates on in the analysis section of his paper.

In addition to data-gathering procedures, a qualitative methods section should also include a description of the analysis procedures, or how the data was coded

(Tracy 2013). The student researcher in this next example received permission to observe communication among children during a school's recess periods:

> After looking at my field notes halfway through my research, I began to interpret my findings and coded them. The three initial groupings I came up with were communication among children, the socially challenged kids, and differences in boys and girls. Once I narrowed down what I was looking for, I continued my fieldwork and soon began to see a pattern. The notes, comments and interpretations from my coded field notes led me to three significant themes amongst the communication of students during recess.

The themes this student refers to at the end of this paragraph are addressed in her analysis section as Boys' Aggressive Communication, Changing Speech Styles Among Others, and Girls' Assertive Communication. While this student probably should have indicated in this paragraph – one of five in her methods section – the titles for her revised themes, the paragraph is still notable for several reasons. First, the description of her analysis process is clear and concise. Second, it provides readers with a transparency that helps bolster her credibility as a researcher; notice that she describes the ongoing process of analysis (including initial categories) rather than pretending the themes she presented in her analysis emerged fully formed.

Again, this is not a how-to methods chapter. If you're writing an empirical research paper you may be writing it for a methods class. Your instructor should provide you with clear guidance on conducting original, data-driven, empirical research. This chapter is offered as guidance on how to *write* each section of the paper regardless of the intricacies of the method you employ. For additional readings that discuss *how to do* quantitative and qualitative research, see the Further Reading section at the end of this chapter.

Reporting Analysis and Findings

Once you've made an argument in your literature review and written a clear and concise description of the methods you employed to gather and analyze your data (keeping in mind that you may revise your literature review after you've gathered and analyzed your data), you will need to report your analysis to your readers. It's important to remember that the *doing* of your analysis and the *writing* of your analysis section are two different processes. Just as in the reporting of methods, the analyses arising from each of the two methodological approaches will be written slightly differently.

Writing the quantitative results and discussion section

The quantitative analysis section, often called Results, will usually consist of reporting the results of the various statistical tests, numerical reporting, and tables of results. The researcher will not necessarily make an argument here, as that would show bias (remember the paradigm in which such studies are under-taken). Instead, these sections are often written in a matter-of-fact tone of voice. Consider this excerpt from a quantitative results section detailing a statistical procedure (correlation) conducted to determine whether one of the researchers' hypotheses, that stress and depression are positively correlated with reports of alcohol consumption among college students, was supported:

> Hypothesis three predicted that stress and depression would be directly associated with participants' drinking behavior. Results of the one-tailed correlations confirmed this relationship for depression, $r(53) = 232$, $p = 047$, but not for stress, $r(53) = -.104$, $p = 230$.
>
> *(Pauley and Hesse 2009, 501)*

Notice a straightforward reporting of the results, in this case from a statistical test called a *correlation*, which shows how strongly two variables are related (Keyton 2014). In other words, the test measures how likely it is that one variable will be significantly present if another variable is also present. In this explanation, the two variables of depression and drinking behavior are strongly correlated. In short, there is some relationship between the two variables where, if one is present, the other is significantly likely to be present as well. As you can tell, writing about complicated statistical relationships like this requires a clear, concise, and direct sentence style.

Writing the qualitative analysis section

While a quantitative results section will be separate from a discussion of those results (a discussion section is often part of quantitative researchers' conclusions), qualitative studies will usually include both reporting and interpretation of data in the same section. For quantitative studies the sections are usually titled "Results" and "Discussion," whereas qualitative studies often have an "Analysis" section. Additionally, if the author has used "I" (or "we" for co-authors) in the beginning of the paper, those pronouns are perfectly acceptable in the analysis section of a qualitative study.

Two students who wrote an ethnography on the way humor communicates a sense of community in stand-up comedy clubs provide a good illustration of the way the reporting of data is linked to analysis. The following excerpt from their paper's analysis section details the fieldwork experience of one of the researchers in a comedy club:

> As a guest in the audience I turn to my right when a woman next to me gestures for my attention, "with only my table in between us I tell her I feel like I will get picked on sitting where I am, and stand out by having a notepad. Laughing, she agrees with me, saying that I will definitely to be picked on during the show" (Field note, 2/18/15). This illustrates the forming of a relationship between audience members. The close proximity of tables allows guests to chat freely and easily. The dialogue shows how two unfamiliar guests create common ground through events that may make them uncomfortable; they are able to find similarity in that

they both find it humorous and thus begin to create a relationship in this community. The communication exchanged between people in the audience illustrates the Uncertainty Reduction Theory, when people set out to find common ground with those of the unknown to reduce possible uncertainties (Griffin et al. 2015, 108). The ability to reduce uncertainty in the formation of a relationship allows for trust, growth, and comfort in the new relationship.

There are several important things to take away from this excerpt in terms of writing a qualitative analysis section. Note the use of "I," which is necessary for the self-reflection (often called "reflexivity") that is a part of writing good field notes (Tracy 2013). Additionally, these authors present an interpretation of their data (their field notes) and frame their interpretation with existing theory. Contrast this with the separation of the two for a quantitative study, as explained earlier in the chapter.

Each type of study has its own conventions of writing regarding the use of the first person and the acceptability of a passive voice. Thinking about these conventions is important, because it sheds light on the expectations of audience members reading that particular type of research. And putting yourself in the reader's place is one of the first steps to making sure your writing is clear. Regardless of the methodological approach, however, you should always use topic sentences and transitions as discussed in Chapter 4.

Conclusions: What Do We Know Now That We Didn't Before?

One of the main questions I ask my students when they begin to write their conclusions is, "What do readers know after finishing your paper that they didn't before reading your paper?" By the time many students reach the conclusions section of their papers, they might feel as though they've said all they need to say. For this reason, many conclusions sections often turn out to be merely a summary of the study itself. While a summary or review is indeed important to include, there are several other important aspects to a conclusions section. Let's consider each of them below, keeping in mind this question: what do readers know after finishing your paper that they didn't when they started reading your paper?

First, let's address the idea of new knowledge. Whether you're doing a quantitative or qualitative study, you've probably already offered some explanations for your data, either in the discussion section or the analysis section. In many quantitative research papers, the discussion section functions as the first part of the conclusions section. In most qualitative research papers, the conclusions are much broader and more wide-ranging than the interpretations offered in the analysis section. Regardless, the conclusions section of your research paper should be the place where you offer your argument(s) as to what your paper – its theories, findings, analysis – means.

For example, the quantitative researchers exploring the link between social support, depression, stress, and drinking among college students concluded the first part of their conclusions section – titled "Discussion" – by speculating on why their data showed that students with low levels of depression and strong social support actually reported *increased* drinking: "In light of the findings from the present study, we can infer that these college women with strong social networks were likely social drinkers whose drinking decisions were fueled by members of their social networks" (Pauley and Hesse 2009, 505). This is new and somewhat surprising knowledge offered by the researchers, potentially contradicting the common-sense notion that college students with strong social support networks and low levels of depression would be *less likely* to report increased drinking.

One of the student-written qualitative pieces described earlier in this chapter provides some interesting conclusions about the role of communication in conflict. When providing some insight into the communication of groups on either side of the divestment movement on his campus, the author noted:

> The layout of an open forum hearing combined with the nonverbal behaviors emitted by participants further escalates the tension felt in the room. The audience mirrors the separation of the debaters in the front of the room by sitting with members from their respective communities. Debaters and audience members alike boisterously respond with an array of nonverbal gestures when they hear the opposing side declare anything they disagree with. Seiter and co-authors (2010) found that when a debater displays nonverbal facial gestures of disapproval while the other debater is speaking, the audience views this debater as being less competent and not as credible as his opponent. These nonverbal behaviors are constantly being implemented by the audience and debaters on stage during an open forum discussion, which further polarizes the two groups to remain dogmatic in their views.

What's surprising here is that we might commonly think of an open forum with a question-and-answer session to be something that might facilitate communication and understanding between groups. But, as this author concludes, it's possible that such forums might only exacerbate the existing divide between groups.

Second, a conclusions or discussion section will typically have a paragraph or two about the limitations of the study and future directions for research, and often the two are combined. For example, you might speculate that a small sample size of only university students for your surveys may have led to inconclusive results and suggest that expanding the sample in future research may yield more significant results. From the earlier example, Pauley and Hesse (2009) conclude that the lack of support for a correlation between stress and drinking behavior might be due to the robustness of their survey instrument:

> In terms of the amount of alcohol participants consumed, depression was correlated with an increase in drinking behavior. The hypothesized correlation between stress and increased alcohol consumption was not supported in

this study. This might be attributable to the fact that reliability estimates for the measure of stress used in this analysis were fairly low. Some recent studies have demonstrated the efficacy of using diaries to track ongoing events like life stress and the amount of affection derived from relationships (Floyd, Hesse, and Pauley 2009). Future studies examining college students' life stress might incorporate such a method to summarize college students' experience with ongoing life stress.

(Pauley and Hesse 2009, 504)

Note that there is a lack of "I" or "we." But there's also a transparency in the authors' tone. While they don't come right out and say, "Maybe we should have picked another survey instrument to use," they do indicate that other instruments might have yielded stronger results. This transparency enhances their credibility as researchers (they can admit the study wasn't perfect) and allows other researchers to build on their study. Certainly, qualitative researchers aren't immune from limitations. In a qualitative study, you might note the need for more interviews or more time in the field. Perhaps something emerged in your observations that you didn't get a chance to follow up on.

Ultimately, and regardless of the methodological approach, any conclusion section to a paper should provide an opportunity to give your readers an "Aha!" moment – some revelation that may alter the way they might normally think about your topic. If you feel that's too much pressure for you when you write your conclusions, no problem. Just try and reach beyond a simple summary of your findings and offer readers a few takeaways. Imagine one of your readers is talking with their friends, and they ask your reader, "What was the point of that paper?" What would you want your reader to tell them? Whatever it is, be sure you write it in your conclusion. Also, since your paper is building on the existing knowledge and research about your paper, suggesting future directions is also a way to contribute to the ongoing dialogue among a community of scholars.

Structure of the Paper: Similarities and Differences

So far, we've discussed the major sections of an empirical research paper, quantitative and qualitative. In either type of paper, you'll usually find an introduction, a literature review, a methods section, an analysis or results section, and a conclusion or discussion section. However, there are some differences that might occur with qualitative empirical papers. These differences, while sometimes small, are important.

These differences might arise if your qualitative paper is more narrative in tone. Narrative research is becoming increasingly popular in social science research (Tracy 2013), and usually falls under the auspices of personal narrative and autoethnography. You might also come across the term "narrative ethnography." What "narrative" means in this sense is *narrating* research, or telling it to readers as you might a story. If this approach interests you, and your instructor has given you the go-ahead, you will need to read many examples to get a feel for this type of writing. There are numerous communication scholars writing in this vein (for examples from just a few, check out some communication articles from: Berry 2016; Boylorn 2013; Chawla 2014; Ellis 2008; Goodall 2006; and Tillman 2015). It's important to keep in mind the "qualitative" caveat; you will not see many narratives in quantitative papers. The reason, if you'll recall our discussion earlier in this chapter, is paradigmatic. If the Post-Positivist paradigm generally eschews "I" and "we" in writing, what are the chances a narrative in which a researcher tells a story will suddenly appear? Slim to none. Of course, this doesn't mean quantitative scholars don't have stories to tell, it just means the writing conventions of that type of research don't allow for them to do so.

The reason I bring this up here is because taking this approach could significantly alter the structure of your paper. For example, if your paper includes a narrative of your research process, your personal life (if it's relevant to your topic), or both, you'll want to give readers some clue *early in your paper* that your voice will be prominent. You don't want to wait until the middle or the end of the paper to offer this voice, as it can be jarring to the reader. Imagine watching a movie about a family that seems to be grounded in the present reality, then, near the end of the movie, a spaceship appears and aliens come to Earth to talk with this family. There's been no hint that this movie was science fiction, or that it took place in a reality in which aliens talk to humans. Now, if this "movie logic" was established early in the film, then this interstellar conversation wouldn't seem out of place. However, if the filmmakers give viewers absolutely no hint that such things are even possible in the reality in which their movie is set, then this scene would seem weird and out of place. This is why you should indicate the presence of a personal narrative in the first few paragraphs.

Let's take a look at the beginning of the student-written paper on comedy, communication, and community cited earlier in this chapter. It starts with a personal narrative that enlightens readers about why one of the researchers is interested in comedy:

> As a young girl I was a complete tomboy! I was in third grade and looked like a sixth grader due to my height. My short bowl cut was sensible to me, but in the shallow culture of my elementary school, I was considered a loser. Since the first day of school I was singled out. Ostracized. I was teased to the point to which I began to hide in bathrooms and eat my meals in the library with the teachers. I would constantly go out of my way to be late to class just so people would not harass me on the way to class. Specifically, there was one boy who was considered the "class clown" who decided I would be his target. After a while, I realized that laughter brought people together, whether it was an innocent joke or a joke at someone else's expense. The laughter is what held the power! At that moment I decided to take control of the situation. I came out of my shell and started to make my fellow classmates laugh as well. I turned humor into something that could create a community and connection with my peers and showed them that funny did not have to be abusive.

Notice that the very first sentence of this paper includes a personal experience written in the first person ("I"). Because of this, readers are not only provided with insight into why one of the researchers is interested in studying comedy, but they are also given concrete examples of the power of humor. The narrative concludes with asterisks that can signal to readers an abrupt jump in tone of voice or time period. In this case, the authors followed their asterisks with a scholarly-sounding introduction similar to what you might expect to read in an academic paper.

If you choose to write a narrative research paper, you'll need to intersperse this voice throughout your paper and at the end as well. Drawing on our previous hypothetical example, it might also seem jarring if a spaceship appeared early on the movie and then the rest of the film played out like a typical family comedy drama. Viewers might wonder, "What happened to the aliens? Are they coming back? Will other spaceships appear?" Obviously, these questions would distract viewers from appreciating the movie itself. The same thing might happen to your readers if you begin with a personal narrative voice and it never reappears in your paper. You definitely don't want your readers to be distracted as they're reading your paper.

One way to ensure that you have a consistent personal narrative throughout your paper is to write your narrative in a separate document. It may be two pages long, or it may be 10 pages long. Then, set that aside and write your empirical research paper. Next, combine the two almost as if you were shuffling a deck of cards, and read it through. Does it make sense? Does it "flow"? You may need to smooth out the transitions. You may want to insert asterisks as in the student example to warn the reader of a transition to your "scholarly" voice (as opposed to your personal voice). Once you look at it as a whole, you may see all the sections of a traditional empirical research paper (introduction, literature review, etc.) interspersed with your own narrative. Of course, you'll need to make sure the paper conforms to your assignment parameters in terms of page length, word count, number of citations, citation style, and anything your instructor requires.

Chapter Summary

This chapter has been a "crash course" on *writing* empirical research papers. It isn't intended as a how-to for any particular method commonly used in the social sciences. Instead, it's meant to offer you some guidance on how you should approach writing empirical research papers, regardless of method. While it's important to remember everything we discussed in Chapter 4 about style and format, realize that each methodological approach will also have its own conventions of writing. For example, most quantitative research papers will be written in the third person and sometimes even in the passive voice. This is because the paradigm in which that research takes place – commonly called Discovery or Post-Positivist – advocates "good science" over a researcher's personal viewpoints, opinions, and biases. Conversely, qualitative research may not only use "I" but also include personal narratives relevant to the research topic.

Regardless of approach, however, there are several sections included with most empirical research papers: introduction (which may also include a justification and rationale for the topic), literature review (we covered the writing of these in Chapter 5, although they'll generally be shorter when part of an empirical research paper), methods, results or analysis, and conclusion or discussion (which may also include limitations on and directions for future research). While the data you gather may not be enough to get your paper accepted at a conference or for publication, it should provide you with a solid foundation on which to build. The next chapter will cover what to with your paper *after* you're done writing it: presenting it and publishing it.

References

Craig, Robert T. 1999. "Communication Theory as a Field." *Communication Theory*, 9: 119–161.

Floyd, Kory, Hesse, Colin, and Pauley, Perry M. 2009. "Writing Affectionate Letters Alleviates Stress: Replication and Extension." Paper presented at the annual conference of the National Communication Association, Chicago, IL.

Fowler, James. 1997. "Moral Stages and the Development of Faith." In *College Student Development and Academic Life: Psychological, Intellectual, Social, and Moral Issues*, edited by Karen Arnold and Ilda Carreiro King, 160–190. New York: Routledge.

Griffin, Em, Ledbetter, Andrew, and Sparks, Glenn. 2015. *A First Look at Communication Theory* (9th ed.). New York: McGraw-Hill.

Keyton, Joanne. 2014. *Communication Research: Asking Questions, Finding Answers*. New York: McGraw-Hill.

Kunzman, Robert. 2012. "How to Talk About Religion." *Educational Leadership*, 69: 44–48.

Merrigan, Gerianne, and Huston, Carole L. 2015. *Communication Research Methods*. New York: Oxford University Press.

Pauley, Perry M., and Hesse, Colin. 2009. "The Effects of Social Support, Depression, and Stress on Drinking Behaviors in a College Student Sample." *Communication Studies*, 60: 493–508.

Pew Forum on Religion and Public Life. (2008). *U.S. Religious Landscape Survey*. Retrieved from http://religions.pewforum.org.

Seiter, J. S., Weger H., Jensen A., and Kinzer, H. J. (2010) "The Role of Background Behavior in Televised Debates: Does Displaying Nonverbal Agreement and/or Disagreement Benefit Either Debater?" *Journal of Social Psychology*, 150: 278–300.

Tracy, Sarah J. 2013. *Qualitative Research Methods: Collecting Evidence, Crafting Analysis, Communicating Impact*. Boston: Wiley.

Further Reading

Berry, Keith. 2016. *Bullied: Tales of Torment, Identity, and Youth*. New York: Routledge.

Boylorn, Robin. 2013. *Sweetwater: Black Women and Narratives of Resilience*. New York: Peter Lang.

Chawla, Devika. 2014. *Home, Uprooted: Oral Histories of India's Partition*. New York: Fordham University Press.

Creswell, John W. 2013. *Research Design: Qualitative, Quantitative, and Mixed Methods Approaches* (4th ed.). Thousand Oaks, CA: Sage.

Dunn, Dana S. 2009. *The Practical Researcher: A Student Guide to Conducting Psychological Research* (2nd ed.). Boston, MA: Wiley-Blackwell.

Ellis, Carolyn. 2008. *Revision: Autoethnographic Reflections on Life and Work*. New York: Routledge.

Ellis, Carolyn, Adams, Tony E., and Bochner, Arthur P. 2011. "Autoethnography: An Overview." *Forum: Qualitative Social Research/Sozialforschung*, 12 (1): Art. 10. Accessed November 14, 2016 from http://www.qualitative-research.net/index.php/fqs/article/view/1589/3095.

Goodall, H. L., Jr. 2006. *A Need to Know: The Clandestine History of a CIA Family*. New York: Routledge.

Keyton, Joanne. 2014. *Communication Research: Asking Questions, Finding Answers*. New York: McGraw-Hill.

Maxwell, Joseph A. 2012. *Qualitative Research Design: An Interactive Approach* (3rd ed.). Thousand Oaks, CA: Sage.

Tillman, Lisa. 2015. *In Solidarity: Friendship, Family, and Activism Beyond Gay and Straight*. New York: Routledge.

8

What Next? Presenting and Publishing Papers

Chapter Learning Outcomes

- Identify competent conference presentation practices
- Distinguish appropriate outlets for publishing papers

Composing Research, Communicating Results: Writing the Communication Research Paper,
First Edition. Kurt Lindemann.
© 2018 John Wiley & Sons, Inc. Published 2018 by John Wiley & Sons, Inc.

Chapter Features

- Engaging Ethics

You've finished writing your paper, you received your grade, and now you're done, right? Only if you want to be. You're probably thinking, "Why *wouldn't* I want to be finished?" Well, sometimes taking your paper beyond the classroom can provide you with valuable experience you can then translate into a career in the public, private, or education sectors. Did you know business consultants (who often have BA, MA, and MS degrees in communication, psychology, and sociology, among other disciplines) often do exactly what you might do with an empirical research paper? They are hired by companies to go into an organization, do research and gather data on a problem, analyze that data, and then write a report for the folks who hired them, offering recommendations that may involve training sessions for employees. Communication trainers, sometimes also consultants, also do research on various issues that people need to improve upon (leadership skills, conflict resolution, working in a diverse environment, etc.) and then present and teach employees those skills.

On the academic side of things, both undergraduate and graduate students may present a shortened version of their class papers at conferences, getting feedback from other professors and academics. This experience, when listed on a curriculum vitae or CV (the academic version of a résumé) can help these students get into graduate school and/or get a teaching position at a college or university. Additionally, they may take the feedback given to them and use it to further revise their paper before submitting to an academic journal, which also looks good when applying to graduate school or for jobs in higher education. In perhaps a more immediate vein, you may be asked by your instructor to present your paper to the class. However, you may find that your instructor has a 10-minute time limit and will not allow you to read your paper verbatim!

In each of the cases above, you're presenting a fairly complex paper in a different medium: speaking instead of writing. Translating your research and analysis from the written to the spoken word requires some forethought, some editing, and some rehearsal. Like many of your professors, I know this routine well, which is why you'll find very few references in this chapter – I have a lot of experience submitting to conferences and journals, and presenting my research in various venues. Many of the things that seem like second nature to your instructors and me, however, are often difficult for others to understand. This concluding chapter explicitly details many of the ins and outs of preparing for conference and journal submissions. It is also designed to help you with the transition from written paper to presentation. Ultimately, this chapter should give you an idea of the multiple ways you can extend the life of that paper you worked so hard to produce.

Presenting Your Paper: Dos and Don'ts

When presenting your paper, you first and foremost need to remember that this is likely the first time your audience will be exposed to your research (unless one or more of your classmates has read a draft prior to your turning it in). The presentation is meant as a "highlight reel" for your paper. You shouldn't expect to present your *entire* paper, regardless of its length. Even if you could read the entire thing, your audience would probably get tired of paying attention and stop listening no matter how interesting it was. Good, close listening takes a lot of work! Below are some points to consider when preparing to present a research paper for an audience.

Content

Our listening attention spans are much shorter than our reading attention spans (Daly 2011). As such, you should be prepared to present a shorter version of your paper containing just the highlights. When paring down your paper for presentation, keep the following in mind:

Do: Condense
- Spend less time on literature reviews and methods.

While you may have put a lot of long hours into researching your topic and gathering your data, your listening audience cares more about what you discovered, uncovered, and can conclude about your topic. So, unless your instructor requires it, condense these two sections to one or two sentences each. The exception to this rule is if the paper you're presenting is solely a literature review.

- Spend more time on findings and conclusions.

Your listening audience wants to know what you found and what it means. And since this is all you'll really have time for in your abbreviated time limit, this is what you should focus on. Of course, you should introduce your topic and tell your audience why it's important they know about your research. But after a 5-minute version of your literature review and methods, get right to the heart of your paper. If you're presenting a literature review, then just focus on your argument and make sure everything else you present is the "Cliff Notes" version of support for that argument.

Do: Give your audience takeaways
When you're done with your presentation, what do you want your audience to remember about your research? Be sure to give them a few "sound bite" takeaways, both in your preview near the beginning of your paper, and in your conclusion.

Don't: Try to present the entire paper
- Be aware of time constraints.

By now you understand why this is the case, but just to reiterate: do not try to present your entire paper, word for word. Instead, gauge how much of your paper you can include, taking care to make your argument or findings and conclusions clear.

Style

The style – or verbal and nonverbal delivery – of your presentations is just as, if not more, important than your content. Now, this isn't a matter of "style over substance." And yet research shows time and again that audiences respond positively to well-delivered presentations (Kawasaki 2010). So, after you've done the work of editing your presentation to fit your assignment requirements and to ensure your audience won't lose interest, you'll need to focus on the delivery of your research.

Do: "Talk the paper"
- Use a conversational style.

You want to the audience to believe you're simply having a conversation with them. This requires you to *sound like* you're having a conversation with them. Notice the emphasis on *sound like*. Of course, this is still a presentation in front of an audience. So, if you normally talk fast in conversations you'll have to slow it down. And if you use a lot of slang when talking to friends, you may have to cut that out as well.

- Cut out verbal filler.

We all use verbal fillers when talking: Um, uh, like, well, and just about any other sound or word we might insert into a pause. Again, while you may do this in conversations, you'll want to try to eliminate them for your presentations. A few are understandable and can even help you sound natural, but more than a couple will be distracting for your audience.

- Get comfortable with silent pauses.

In the United States and many Western countries, we're especially wary of silence (Daly 2011). So, when the time comes for a pause in our presentations, it usually seems weird and interminably long; if we're in front of people giving a speech, sound should be coming out of our mouth at all times, right? Not quite. First, pauses always seem longer to the speaker than to the audience. Second, audiences need time to think about what you've said; pauses can facilitate reflection on the part of the audience. Third, pauses can be used to emphasize crucial points. Pausing right after or right before an important sentence can communicate to audiences, "This is important."

- All of the above means rehearsing the paper.

The only way to get good at modulating your tone (high and low) and rate (fast and slow), and get comfortable with pauses is to rehearse your presentation. Too often, people look at their notecards or presentation script while silently reading it over again and again, and call it "rehearsing."

Athletes don't kick or hit a ball for the very first time during an actual game; they do it in practice again and again. Presenting should be no different. First, speak your presentation out loud. Each time, try to read less and less from your paper or notecards. The more you do this, the more conversational you will sound. Second, plan out where to pause. Doing this will help you to remain silent during a 2- or 3-second pause. Third, time yourself. You want to be sure that you have about a 10-second cushion with you speaking comfortably and conversationally, with the planned pauses throughout.

Don't: Read the paper

By now this should go without saying, but don't read your paper in its entirety. Of course, there may be sections of your paper you want to read verbatim. This often happens with reaction and application papers, as well as rhetorical analyses, in which passages from the artifact (a speech, advertisement, film, etc.) need to be quoted aloud so audiences can get a sense of the language you're examining. Similarly, you may have written a description of a scene from the film you're examining, and you've put careful work into the writing of this description. In this case as well, you should read it verbatim.

Reading passages verbatim is also important when presenting qualitative research projects. You may have written a thoughtful description of an observation in your field notes and included it in your paper, and your audience may get a better sense of your analysis as a whole by hearing it in its entirety. In the same vein, the actual words participants spoke in an interview can be powerful for an audience and give audience members a fuller picture of your data, thereby helping them better understand your analysis.

Besides the above examples, however, reading your paper aloud is often a recipe for a poor presentation. Granted, some people can do this and make it sound natural, but developing the skills noted in the first part of this chapter can help you in other areas of public speaking: impromptu speaking, in particular, for which you use no notes and speak "off the top of your head." Overall, this section was meant to offer you some guidelines on translating your paper to a presentation. There are many excellent textbooks on public speaking. Chances are you may have already read one for a communication class you were required to take. For more tips, guidelines, and exercises designed to help you become a better public speaker, reference any of those textbooks.

Visual aids

You may have access to technology that allows you to use visual aids to supplement your presentation. As with the preparation and delivery of your presentation, there are a few dos and don'ts to keep in mind.

Do: Rehearse with your visual aids

Regardless of what your visual aids consist of – film clips, physical movement, PowerPoint slides, professional-looking poster boards – you should rehearse your presentation while using your visual aids so you can be sure you won't run over your time limit. Getting familiar enough with visual aids to seamlessly integrate them into your presentation takes time, and not being familiar with them *during* your presentation can take time away from what you intend to tell your audience. So, be sure to create your visuals aids keeping in mind that they must: (a) be easy to use; (b) not take up more time than they should; and (c) not distract you or your audience from the content of your presentation. This last point is particularly important for the most common type of visual aid, PowerPoint and/or Prezi slides, and is related to the next guideline.

Do: Make sure your visual aids enhance rather than detract

Remember that the goal of visual aids is to *enhance* your presentation. Everything on your slides (PowerPoint, Prezi, or other software), any film clip, or any physical object you use should be minimally incorporated into your presentation so that it enhances what you are already telling your audience. For example, putting an entire section of your presentation on a PowerPoint slide is distracting; it encourages audience members to read what you've written instead of listening to you. In general, effective uses of visual aids in the form of slides, regardless of software, include reinforcing your arguments and reorienting your audience to your topic.

Reinforcement   Use your visual aids to reiterate what you've already verbally stated. It sounds bad to be redundant, but in this case appealing to your audience through your words and images on a screen can go a long way toward making sure your audience gets your point and leaves your presentation with something to think about. Reinforcing what you're saying with words or images on a screen counters the short attention span most audiences have nowadays by not asking audience members to rely solely on their listening skills to get your point.

Another way to use visual aids to reinforce your point is to lay out your organizational structure in written form. Including a slide with the topic sentence of that particular point can serve as an internal signpost, letting the audience know exactly where you are in your presentation. Notice that I suggest putting a topic sentence on the slide. While it's sometimes effective to have a word or phrase to minimally reinforce your points for your audience, it's also useful to make that slide persuasive in nature. Your topic sentence, since it's part of your argument, might be a good choice in this respect.

Reorientation   Making your slides persuasive in tone can also help your audience reorient their attitude toward a particular topic. Yes, your visual aids should be minimal in the sense that they don't present *new* information you don't already have in the verbal script for your presentation. However, this doesn't mean that visual aids can't be persuasive. For example, a presentation about inflammatory anti-gay rhetoric might benefit from a graph showing growing rates of violence toward the LGBTQ (lesbian, gay, bisexual, transgender, queer) community. The audience can better visualize the potential harms of such hate speech. This slide might also have a title like "Rising Rates of LGBTQ Violence." Yes, the title is descriptive, but in the larger context of your presentation it can also be persuasive in the sense that it helps support your overall claim, whether it's a claim of fact, value, or policy.

Don't: Let your visual aids do all the work

That said, you want to be sure you don't let your visual aids do all the work for you. As implied in earlier sections on visual aid use, putting every word of your presentation on a PowerPoint slide is simply poor practice. If the goal of your presentation was for your audience to read your paper, you would just hand it to them and leave the room – no presentation needed! And if your slides are poorly designed – too many words, awkward color scheme, too much animation, irrelevant images – you've violated the first "do" of this section, that your visual aids should enhance not detract from your speech. For more on designing visual aids slides and using them effectively in presentations, see the Further Reading section at the end of this chapter.

Don't: Assume everyone has the same access and abilities

Some of your audience members may not be able to easily read your visual aids, if at all. If you have advance notice, you can make your slides accessible for screen-reading devices and make them available to your audience ahead of time. Making PowerPoint slides screen-reader accessible requires you to follow certain guidelines for constructing slides, including font, color scheme, and slide layout choices (Disability Access Services 2014). See this link from the State of California's Department of Rehabilitation for more information on creating accessible slides: http://www.dor.ca.gov/disabilityaccessinfo/das-docs/7-steps-2-create-accessible-powerpoint-slideshow.pdf.

In addition to creating screen-reader-friendly slideshows to distribute in advance, you might simply put the text for your slides into a Word document. Distributing this document in advance will also help those with differing abilities to access your slideshow. Exporting to a pdf document may also be an option. Check with your university's instructional technology staff or disability center for more tips, guidelines, and suggestions. If you're not able to distribute slides in advance, offer to make them available after your presentation for any interested audience members.

In summary, remember that a paper presentation doesn't have to be a presentation of the *entire* paper. Unless your class assignment requires you to read your paper to the class, you should conversationally talk through your paper to your audience, reading verbatim *only* those parts you think will *absolutely* help the audience better understand your research and will not make you go over your time limit. And the only way you will know whether your content and delivery – pauses, conversational tone, reading parts verbatim – will put you over your allotted time limit is by *rehearsing*.

Conferences and conventions

It's easy to understand why you would want to give an excellent presentation when presenting in a class: you'll likely get a good grade. But what about presentations that aren't graded? Why would someone ever want to do those? Presenting at conferences, whether they are local, regional, national, or international, can provide you with valuable experience in innumerable ways. For some undergraduate and graduate students, this means getting feedback on papers, inspiration for other research projects, and networking. If you do present your paper at a conference, some of the people you'll be presenting to could be your future employers, professors, and colleagues; you'll want to be sure to make a good impression. Following the guidelines for presentations we previously covered will go a long way toward creating the best possible impression for your audiences.

Academic conference formats can vary, but most have the same major components. If your paper is accepted for submission, you are placed on a *panel* with other presenters who have written about related topics. You are required to send your *respondent* (a person tasked with providing an oral and sometimes written response to each presenter during the panel) and/or *chair* (a moderator of the panel, making sure everyone adheres to time limits and audience members have a chance to ask questions) a version of your paper well before the conference. Sometimes the respondent and chair are the same person. Whether you send your original submission or a revised one (this is sometimes permissible), you should plan to send the most current version of your paper to the respondent and chair at least one month prior to your presentation date. During the panel, each person will present (usually for about 10 minutes), after which time the respondent or moderator will offer some unifying thoughts for the audience and perhaps some individual feedback to each of the presenters. The audience will then be allowed to ask questions and make comments. In total, a panel could run from an hour to an hour and a half. Since you will be registered for the conference, you will be free to attend any other events (panels, book fairs, keynote speeches, receptions) you wish. There is usually a convention program, often online and in booklet form, that will help you decide which events to attend. These events are great places to meet other students and scholars from other universities.

Submitting to conferences is more a matter of careful preparation and attention to detail than majorly revising your class paper or starting a new paper from scratch. Of course, if you write a paper for one of your classes and your instructor recommends you submit it to a conference, you should seriously consider both your instructor's recommendation *and* the feedback they provide on your paper. Your teachers are grading *a lot* of papers and presentations, so the fact that they took time to write such encouraging words shouldn't be taken as false praise. Further, even if your instructor doesn't explicitly say it, their recommendation is probably based on your revising the paper as per their comments. While your paper doesn't have to be perfect for you to submit it to a conference, it should be free of typos and grammatical errors, and adhere to the page length specified in the call for papers (CFP) for that particular conference.

Paying attention to the guidelines in the CFP for a conference is important. Usually, the bigger regional and national conferences have divisions for each area of study. For example, the American Psychological Association has divisions in clinical, educational, and health psychology, along with many others. In the field of communication, the National Communication Association has divisions for rhetoric, and interpersonal, intercultural, organizational, and health communication, among other areas. The CFPs for these divisions will require a specific citation style and page length. So, you should have an idea of where you're going to submit before you revise to be sure you're not wasting your time by lengthening your paper when you really should be cutting it down.

If you are interested in submitting to a conference, it's always best to ask an instructor (from the class for which you wrote the paper, or another one with whom you feel comfortable) if they would be willing to look over your revisions. If you ask the instructor who gave you the initial feedback, they will already be familiar with your paper and probably won't have to spend a lot of time rereading it. But before you can do that, you'll need to decide which conference you might want to submit to.

There are a lot of factors to consider when choosing an academic conference. The most obvious one is the academic discipline in which you're working. While it may make sense to submit a paper written for a communication class to a communication conference, a paper in sociology to a sociology conference, etc., there isn't a hard and fast rule. For example, your paper may address a topic or use theories that are appropriate for a psychology conference even though you wrote it in a communication class. As always, your instructor or another professor is the best person to ask.

Cost is something else to consider. Depending on the conference and its location, attending a conference can be expensive: travel (driving or flying), hotel room, registration, and meals all must be factored in. Sometimes, your department may cover some or all of your costs; it never hurts to ask. Often, departments are proud to showcase the research of their undergraduate and graduate students, and may be willing to find at least some money to defray costs.

You also need to consider your own schedule. Instructors may allow you to miss class for academic reasons; but they may not. Can you afford to take time off school, work, family and relationship obligations? These are all important questions. And you must ask yourself them *before* submitting, as it's considered bad form to submit something, have it accepted, and then choose not to attend; your paper being accepted means someone else's paper may not have gotten accepted, and the other person may have been willing and able to attend whereas you've decided not to attend. All in all, attending and presenting at a conference, while a valuable experience, is also a sacrifice. However, the benefits of feedback and networking with like-minded people usually outweigh the financial costs and time commitments.

Local and regional

Often, the cheapest and easiest conferences to attend are those right in your own "backyard." Local conferences, especially if you live or go to school in a tourist-destination city, may be an annual occurrence – and you may not even know it. Local and regional conferences are usually the best places for a student scholar to submit and present their work.

University research symposiums One easy-to-attend conference is one at your own or a neighboring university. Many universities host research symposia and competitions for their undergraduate and graduate students. For example, San Diego State University hosts its Student Research Symposium (http://srs.sdsu.edu/) every year, which highlights research from undergraduates, Masters, and doctoral students. Faculty and professionals from the area volunteer to judge poster and oral presentations, and the top students receive cash awards. It costs nothing to enter, but does require thorough preparation. Check and see if your school or department hosts such a conference. A neighboring school might also host a conference to which you can submit. The benefits of attending and presenting at these conferences are many: little to no travel, no cost, and no extra meal money required.

The drawbacks, while fewer, are also worth considering. First, while you may meet other graduate students and professors from other areas, you may not have the networking opportunities you would at a regional or national conference. Second, you may not get feedback on your paper from a truly unbiased moderator, judge, or respondent. The people providing feedback may already know you or even be your professors. Finally, because you're in familiar surroundings, with some familiar faces, you may not be faced with the same pressure you would be at a less local conference. While you certainly don't want to feel anxious, "real-world" presentation situations – in which you're stating opinions and arguments to others you don't know and being evaluated on your presentation – can be much different from classroom assignments. Presenting at your own university, while a great start, may not simulate such situations as much as other conferences would.

State associations   A bigger conference can be held by a state academic association. For example, in the United States, Florida has the Florida Communication Association Annual Convention (http://floridacom.org/). The Connecticut Psychological Association also has an annual convention (http://connpsych.org/). And the Hawaii Sociological Association has an annual meeting (https://sites.google.com/site/hawaiisociology/home). Not all states have academic associations in every discipline, nor an annual convention, so be sure to check. If you're lucky enough to be in a state with an association, then submitting can be another opportunity to network and present your research.

As you might guess, there are endless possibilities for conference presentations in a variety of disciplines. Rather than enumerate all of them, I provide a more narrow view of conferences in the rest of the chapter. Specifically, I cover the major conference opportunities in the field of communication. As always, ask your instructor or another professor in your department for their feedback and advice on conferences and submissions.

Regional communication associations   In the communication discipline, regional conferences are a great way for undergraduate and graduate students to get familiar with academic gatherings and presentation formats. In the United States there are four major regional communication conventions: Western States Communication Association (WSCA, at http://www.westcomm.org/), Southern States Communication Association (SSCA, at http://www.ssca.net/), Central States Communication Association (CSCA, at http://www.csca-net.org/aws/CSCA/pt/sp/home_page), and Eastern Communication Association (ECA, at http://www.ecasite.org/aws/ECA/pt/sp/p_Home_Page). Anyone from any region (or country) is welcome to submit to any of the four, though undergraduate and graduate students may find it less expensive and less demanding on school schedules to attend a conference in their own region.

Other than a potentially close-to-home location, there are a few aspects that make regional conferences a great place to start. Regional conferences, while larger in attendance than local or university-based conferences, are still small enough to avoid feeling overwhelmed by the number of panels and participants. As such, these conventions usually offer more opportunities to speak with other students and scholars in a less hectic environment. Perhaps more importantly to students, registration costs are often lower than national and international conventions, as are the travel and lodging costs.

National and international

Many scholars will go to more than one academic conference a year, and in the communication discipline the two largest ones are the National Communication Association Annual Convention (https://www.natcom.org/convention/) and the International Communication Association Annual Conference (https://www. icahdq.org/conf/index.asp). Just as there are benefits and drawbacks to attending local and regional conferences, each of these national conventions has advantages and disadvantages to submitting, attending, and presenting.

As with each of the types of conferences previously mentioned, what is one person's advantage in attending may be another person's disadvantage, and vice versa. These conferences (NCA and ICA) are massive, boasting upwards of 2,000 participants, and are held in major cities in order to accommodate these numbers, which means lodging will often be more expensive than for the regional conferences. Bigger conferences potentially mean bigger cities that may offer more to see and do than the smaller cities regional conferences are sometimes held in, if you like a vibrant metro area, its nightlife, and cultural attractions. What's more, the ICA conference is held an international location every four years. Although the cost could be significantly higher than for U.S. conferences, it affords a great opportunity to travel abroad.

Of course, bigger conferences also mean meeting and networking with more people from a wider spectrum of academia and, sometimes, the non-profit and private sectors. You can potentially make more connections than you might at a regional conference, and certainly than at a local or university-hosted conference. If you're interested in attending a particular graduate school and/or living in a certain region of the country, going to a national convention like the NCA or ICA conferences may help you make those all connections in one place rather than attending conferences in every region in which you'd like to live.

A final advantage and disadvantage for these national and international conventions is that there is a division for nearly every subdiscipline imaginable in the field of communication. A *division* is a group of individuals who have formed a special organization within the larger one that focuses on a particular area of interest or methodological approach. These can range from more established foci like rhetoric, interpersonal, media, and organizational communication to newer ones like sport communication. This is an advantage for you because chances are, whatever the focus of your paper you can find a division that your paper fits. A disadvantage may be that you become overwhelmed with number of choices. Ask your instructor or another professor if you're not sure.

Subject- and method-specific conventions   As if those weren't enough conferences to consider, there are also a number of more focused conferences for which your paper might also be appropriate. These conventions can range from a focus on a particular method to an area of research. Listed below are the sponsoring organizations for each respective gathering. The cost for registration and travel varies, so be sure to check each website for specifics.

- *International Congress of Qualitative Inquiry* (http://icqi.org/). This annual conference draws scholars from all over the world and is focused on the critical qualitative study of social justice issues from a variety of disciplines and perspectives.
- *International Association for Relationship Research Mini and Main Conferences* (http://www.iarr.org/). From its website, this organization is "a scientific and professional organization including hundreds of scholars and practitioners focused on stimulating and supporting the scientific study of personal and social relationships" (para. 1). They have several smaller conferences and one main conference.
- *Rhetoric Society of America Biennial Conference* (http://associationdatabase. com/aws/RSA/pt/sp/home_page). This is an organization for "scholars, teachers and students interested in the study of rhetoric ... which includes spoken, written, visual and material texts circulating in a wide variety of situations" (para. 1). It holds a conference every two years.
- *Organizational Communication Mini-Conference*. This is a free, student-focused conference that centers on the study of organizational communication and rotates to various college campuses across the United States. It does not have one specific home institution or website.

When submitting to a conference like those of the NCA, ICA, or WSCA, there are a few things you can do (besides having a well-written paper) to increase your chances of acceptance. First, conferences like to encourage student participation, so be sure to put "STUDENT SUBMISSION" on your submission. This might go on the title page, in the electronic form for submissions, and on the header for each page. Besides this, you will have to omit any identifying information so the reviewers don't know who the author is. This is called an *anonymous review*. Second, since you and your classmates are the future scholars and teachers of your discipline, conferences want to encourage you to present. As such, most conventions have created a special "DEBUT PAPER" designation you can also put on your title page, electronic form, or header. This simply means that this is your first ever submission to that particular conference. These two labels can increase your chance of acceptance, as reviewers see these designations and usually evaluate papers as they would with a beginning student scholar and not as they would with an established scholar. Always check the call for papers for each conference to find out the details.

Engaging Ethics

Besides plagiarism, which we've already covered in previous chapters, there are a few ethical guidelines to follow with conference submissions. I've listed two of them below.
- *If you've already presented a paper at a regional or national conference, you should not present the same paper at another conference.*
  As scholars often study the same topic as an overarching research agenda, you can certainly present a different paper on a related topic, just not the *exact* same paper. College-specific research symposiums are generally considered to be exempt from this rule.

- *If you have published a paper, you cannot submit it to present at a conference.* The reasoning behind this is that publication is thought to be the pinnacle of exposure for your paper, with everything else (class assignment and conference paper) considered stages leading up to publication. Sometimes, people may submit for conferences and publication more or less simultaneously, which is generally permissible. However, it's certainly acceptable to bypass conferences and simply submit your paper for publication.

Publishing

So, you've written and revised your class paper, and submitted and presented it at conference. Up to this point, your classmates may have read it or heard you present it, and you may have presented it to an audience at a conference. Hopefully, the feedback you received has given you some ideas about how, where, and why you should refine it even further. In fact, depending on how active your teacher or other academic mentor has been in helping you revise your paper, you may want to consider adding them as a co-author on your paper (a common practice in academia). Regardless, if you want to put this feedback into practice, your next step is to submit it for publication.

If you thought there were a lot of conference choices while reading the previous section, you'll definitely be overwhelmed with the number of journals it might be appropriate to submit your paper to. For example, in the field of communication, each major organization noted above has several journals associated with it, and each regional association publishes at least one academic journal. Additionally, several of the topic- or method-focused associations publish at least one journal. And those are just communication-specific journals; if we widen the possibilities to other journals outside of your own discipline or major, there are enough journal titles to fill an entire chapter of this book. Suffice it to say, check with your instructor or another professor in your home department for advice. This rest of this chapter will be devoted to offering some general guidelines for preparing to submit your paper for publication.

Where should you publish?

This is a difficult question to answer even for scholars who are already published. The first step, besides asking an experienced scholar, is to read a few articles from a journal you're thinking about submitting to. You should already have read some academic articles for your classes and, especially, for those articles you cited in your paper (don't just read the abstract and cite it!). If not, then that's the first place to start. In either case, you must not only become familiar with the format of academic articles, you must understand the kinds of articles that are published by particular journals.

In addition, you can do other things to ensure your piece fits with the editorial direction of the journal. Read the editorial mission (available online with all journals). Consider how your paper dialogues with other published articles: Does your article address similar concerns to other published pieces? Does it fall in line with the methods employed by other published articles? Go back to your own paper.

Are there certain authors you cite frequently? Where did they publish those pieces? That journal might be a starting place for your submission as well.

After you submit and your paper has been reviewed, there are four decisions you might receive. These decisions are: Accept (yay!), Accept with Minor Revisions (yay!), Revise and Resubmit (yay!), and Reject (boo!). Notice that the first three decisions should all be considered positively. An outright *acceptance* with no revisions is rare, and an *accept with minor revisions* is more common. Both mean your piece is accepted for publication, though you'll probably have to do some revisions to satisfy the concerns of the editor and reviewers. A *revise and resubmit* decision means the editor and reviewers can't accept the article as it is, but may reconsider if you complete some substantial revisions. Of course, a *reject* decision is just like it sounds. If your piece gets rejected, no big deal. Award-winning, prolific scholars get rejections from journals all the time. The trick is to not give up. So, look at the feedback and revisions to determine if there's anything you should think about revising again. At this point, you may be sick of revising the article, so there's nothing wrong with simply submitting it to another journal as is provided there are no glaring errors. After all, you may receive a *revise and resubmit* from the second journal and will end up revising it a different way anyway.

When you submit, you should expect a fairly long wait. It's not unusual for three or more months to pass before a journal editor renders a decision to an author; and that's considered a timely response! In total, it can take up to a year from submission to acceptance to publication, when you see your article in print. And the readership for those journals might be small compared to other types of outlets (magazines, websites). This is why many academic scholars continue to advocate for other outlets for academic writings. In the communication and sociology disciplines, for example, writers and researchers like Arthur Bochner, Carolyn Ellis, Patricia Leavy, Katherine Miller, and Sarah Tracy, among others, have all advocated in various outlets for writing for more "mainstream audiences" (those outside their respective academic disciplines). However, in academia writ large, publication in these *peer-reviewed journals* is, rightly or wrongly, generally considered more prestigious than more "mainstream" publications to people who make decisions about admittance to graduate school, hiring, tenure, and promotion. This attitude is slowly changing, but if you're pursuing a graduate degree or, eventually, a position in a college or university, academic journals might be your best bet for now.

There are some journals solely devoted to undergraduate and graduate student research; those might be a good place to start, but another strategy is to start at the top and work your way down. In other words, find out from your advisor or mentor the *best* journal in your particular discipline. Submit your polished paper and hope for the best. If you get rejected, submit your piece to the next most prestigious journal, and so on.

Chapter Summary

In this chapter we've covered some dos and don'ts of presenting academic papers to audiences, and why you might want to do so in the first place. There are many venues available should you want to submit to a conference, and the same goes for submitting your papers for publication. In each case, it's important to remember that your instructors are often the best resource for advice and guidance. That said, sometimes the authors of the very articles you cite in your own paper might be willing to offer you some advice as well. Students sometimes feel hesitant to contact the scholarly authors they've read, but usually these scholars are happy to hear from an interested reader; it helps remind them that people are reading and thinking about their ideas.

Whatever course you pursue, you should have confidence in your work while remembering that there's always room for improvement. Conference presentations and journal submissions are useful for feedback, and such feedback is usually given with the best of intentions and not to make the author feel bad. In either case, good writing takes practice. So, put your best effort into your papers with the desire to improve and you will improve. Good luck!

References

Daly, John A. 2011. *Advocacy: Championing Ideas and Influencing Others.* New Haven, CT: Yale University Press.

Disability Access Services. 2014. "Seven Steps to Creating an Accessible PowerPoint Slideshow." Accessed June 12, 2016 from http://www.dor.ca.gov/disabilityaccessinfo/das-docs/7-steps-2-create-accessible-powerpoint-slideshow.pdf.

Kawasaki, Guy. 2010. *Enchantment: The Art of Changing Hearts, Minds, and Actions.* New York: Portfolio/Penguin.

Further Reading

Reynolds, Garr. 2012. *Presentation Zen: Simple Ideas on Presentation Design and Delivery.* Berkeley, CA: New Riders.

Tufte, Edward R. 2006. *The Cognitive Style of PowerPoint: Pitching Out Corrupts Within.* Cheshire, CT: Graphics Press.

Index

Composing Research, Communicating Results: Writing the Communication Research Paper,
First Edition. Kurt Lindemann.
© 2018 John Wiley & Sons, Inc. Published 2018 by John Wiley & Sons, Inc.